MW00682853

WIT, WILL & ANGELS

One Life of a Woman in the 20th Century

To Spirus
with many good wishes!
Dorothea Klassen

Jan. 31, 2015

© 2014 Dorothea Klassen
All Rights Reserved
FIRST EDITION

No part of this publication may be reproduced, stored in a
retrieval system, or transmitted in any form or by any means,
electronic, mechanical, photocopying, recording or otherwise,
without the written permission of the author.

Published by Crunch! Inc. Communications
568 South River Road
Elora, ON N0B 1S0
www.crunchcommunications.com

*Additional maps and photographs can be viewed at Dorothea's website,
where you can also purchase a copy of this book.*
www.dorotheaklassen.com

To my sons

CONTENTS

Foreword   vii

Preface   ix

1   A Journey Begins: Early Days in Germany   1

2   War Years as a Teenager   31

3   Life as an Apprentice on a State Farm   43

4   Escape from Brietzig   48

5   First Return to Thurow   62

6   Leaving Thurow a Second Time   71

7   Becoming a Landowner   82

8   We Break for the Black Border   92

9   Life on the Other Side   129

10 Goodbye to Germany   148

11 Beginning Life in Canada   159

12 Settlers in Toronto   173

13 A Teaching Career   181

14 Spiritual and Worldly Journeys   202

Photographs & Maps   105

Acknowledgements   215

About the Author   217

how rare
  that stars extend
  their long and slender fingers
          from a dark and boundless ceiling

mysterious touch...
  illuminates the highways
              which arranged this happy meeting

FOREWORD

~

As a teenager, I spent many a late night sitting at the edge of my mother's bed, as we both puzzled over one or another of life's mysteries, the day's events, future plans, dreams, other people, or just growing up. I think I discovered that my mom was cool earlier than most kids, although this surely did not happen while she was a teacher in the same elementary school I attended. Thank goodness I was never in her class. Calling her Mrs. Klassen would have been weird.

She started seeming cool to me when she took my side in high school, opposing the administrators, like me, although for entirely different reasons. Catholic boys' schools in the mid-1960s were quite unlike today. Hair that went beyond collar length was grounds for a summons to the disciplinarian's office. When I was told to get a haircut and "don't come back until you do", the fact that I was a member of a fledgling rock and roll band held no sympathy or sway. Readers can probably guess what did not happen next.

Three days later, when my schoolteacher mother came home for some reason at mid-day and I was just getting out of bed, I greeted her cheerily. Naturally she wanted to know why I was not at school. When I explained that I did not want to get a haircut, she became annoyed, surprisingly, not at me. She drove to the school and gave the principal an earful for not notifying her or enquiring about my absenteeism or whereabouts. I did agree, after some urging, to a haircut compromise. It appeared the disciplinarian had, in turn, been given a talking-to by the principal. When I did finally return to school, he called me to his office and said simply, "I meant for you to go to the barbershop down the street." I believe I responded, "But Sir, you didn't say that."

That was my mom. She didn't always understand or agree with what I or my brother did or decided, but she always supported whatever that was. She allowed us to succeed.

Those teenage years were certainly seminal in my life. Mother introduced me to the spirituality that existed in the trees and the wind and sky and inside me and all people, all of which was becoming increasingly self-evident to me at that time. While I experimented with various substances popular with my peers, she helped put my insights into perspective, making sense of them, and bringing a spiritual discipline to my thinking through books and teachings like Self Realization Fellowship (SRF) and the Bible, which I read from beginning to end while on the road with the band.

I did not know the full story of my mother's early life until she started writing it down, several years after her retirement. I was certainly aware of some of her harrowing experiences in 1945, but it was the context of growing up in that transformative time I never understood until I read these pages. Her earliest years—as a young girl and a teenager, growing up in an agricultural society verging on the discovering of electricity and motorized vehicles—defined her. They gave her the strength to overcome obstacles which in later life must at times have seemed trivial by comparison. She is a witness to a Century of change, with it's myriad evolving problems, technologies, politics and relationships, and has acquired a perspective on life that is truly unmatched in any other individual I know.

As I write this, Mother is 89. We are still working on her story, and I guess, now, it is ready to be shared. I hope you enjoy reading it as much as I feel favoured for having been a part of it.

Garrett Klassen
Easter Sunday, 2014

PREFACE

~

Many books have been written about the events of the Twentieth Century. Every historical writer brings his or her own interpretation and understanding to the script, especially when those writers rely on hearsay and the written reports of others. Actual events can be reported only insofar as they are experienced by the observer, and it is well accepted that any two observers, seeing the same event, may describe it from completely different points of view, making it appear almost contradictory.

This autobiography describes my life; a life of one of many women who were born in the first quarter of the Twentieth Century, who experienced a childhood of war and confusion, and the violence that reigned down upon their little village, upon all of central Europe, and beyond. It is the story of the miracles and many small wonders that helped me survive, that brought me to Canada, and that finally made me a citizen of the world and of the Universe.

It is through these eyes that I hope the reader will share my joys and tribulations, as I walk through the passages of my life.

My journey begins in a village in the eastern part of Germany, where life has not changed much since the Middle Ages. There is no electricity, water is pumped by hand from a well in the yard, the street is a dirt road, dusty in the summer, muddy in spring and fall and icy in winter. My father, a newcomer and master electrician, is an instrumental figure in bringing about modernization and change. My mother, a former school teacher, provides a happy and harmonic family life in which my younger brother and I are lucky to grow from childhood into our teenage years.

When World War II begins, life changes; slowly at first but inevitably it affects my young life and alters the lives of my family members forever. It is this first passage into maturity, more than any other that follows, which defines for me the instinctive choice between fight or flight, swim or sink, live or die.

I chose all three: to fight, to swim and to live.

A second passage begins for me as a twenty-year-old girl, in a different, post-war environment. New challenges and hurdles must be overcome, and again, life-changing decisions must be made. Having survived by my wits, determination and a will to succeed, at age 29, together with my new husband and infant son, we decide to immigrate to Canada.

A different world opens up for me here; less physically dangerous, but challenging, exciting, adventurous and filled with unbelievable opportunities that have only to be grasped. Canada becomes my life success story.

Looking back at my life, now in my 80s, I am contented and happy, and I realize how much reason I have to be grateful for the wisdom that life's "hard knocks" have taught me.

I remain the girl who believes she always found herself in the right place at the right time—not just for a convenient bit of luck, but for survival. I have been blessed to be able to hear and follow the guidance of a higher power. May each reader be so fortunate to listen to this silent voice, which dwells within us all.

Maria-Dorothea Klassen
Mississauga, Ontario

WIT, WILL
& ANGELS

Four generations of Hildebrandts:
Great-grandmother, grandmother, mother and child.

CHAPTER ONE

A Journey Begins: Early Days in Germany

I re-entered the world on January 30th, 1925, in Stettin, Pommerania—or Pommern—Germany, and was named Maria-Dorothea Hartmann but became known only as Doerte Hartmann. In Canada everyone calls me Dorothea. I decided to use this name here because the pronunciation of Doerte in English sounds too much like "dirty".

Because life in Canada is so completely different from the experiences of my youth and those during the Second World War in Germany, I wish to tell my story, or at least some of the highlights of my life to those who might like to listen.

At the time of my birth, my parents lived in a little village called Brietzig, which was located about 50 kilometres southeast of Stettin (*pronounced Shtetteen*) in the county of Pyritz, and about an equal distance away from the Baltic Sea.

My parents, Waldemar Hartmann and Margarete Hildebrandt, had married on July 27th, 1923, in Stettin where my mother's parents lived. My mother had been a teacher since about 1917, at first in a small village and then in the town of Pyritz, which had about 10,000 inhabitants. She had been engaged during the First World War to a young man with the last name of Neumann, but he was killed in action. An aunt of my mother lived nearby in Brietzig, and it was during one of her visits to this aunt that she met my father.

The aunt was the mother of the local miller, Emil Naumann. One day, as my mother was sitting with a basket full of newly hatched chicks in front of the mill, my father happened to pass by and started a conversation with her. She must have made a lasting impression on him, for they had a very happy and harmonious marriage, though not without heartbreaks and tough times. At that time women did not go out to work after they were married, so my mother moved with my father to Brietzig.

My father was born in Penzig, a village in Schlesien—or Selesia—which was carved off Germany and given to the Poles after the war ended in 1945. The river Niesse became the new border and the nearby city of Goerlitz remained part of East Germany.

Like my mother, he was born in 1895. He had been drafted as a young man into the army during the First World War and had fought on the Eastern Front, mainly in Macedonia, where he contracted malaria. I remember at least two attacks that he suffered during my childhood.

After the war, Waldemar boarded with his married sister, Else, in Berlin. There, my father became an electrician apprentice, soon a journeyman and then a Master Electrician. This meant that he had passed several examinations and was now eligible to train apprentices himself and open his own business. As a young boy, he had learned to appreciate classical music and to play the violin. Now, during his stay in Berlin, he visited the Opera and concerts as often as his time allowed.

At the beginning of the 1920s very few people had electric light, let alone stoves or farm machinery. My father had decided to find an area in the country where he could be the person to bring electricity to the various farm communities. Such a place he found near Pyritz—one of the richest farmers' villages around. Brietzig is about 10 kilometres east of Pyritz and it was located on the narrow gauge train route that ran between Pyritz and Ploenzig until the end of the Second World War.

There was no other electrician far and wide except for my father, so he became extremely busy, working in at least fifteen to twenty villages, putting electrical equipment into the farm operations. I remember that at first he always travelled on his bicycle, and later, on a small motorcycle which we referred to as "minimax". If large equipment had to be used, the farmers came with their horse-drawn wagons and picked it up, but I can still see him, often having large rolls of wiring wrapped around his shoulder and bags of tools around his waist, getting on his minimax and riding off with lots of noise and exhaust fumes trailing behind.

One of my earliest memories is a trip with him on this tread motorcycle to a neighbouring *Gutshaus*: a huge Manor House in which the landlord—the "lord of the surrounding land"—lived. In this case it belonged to an elderly lady, whose mansion my father equipped with electricity. I was about four years old and remember how kind she was to me and how I was allowed to walk through the big fancy rooms. Two years later, when my father bought our house, in which we had previously occupied the upstairs flat, she gave us one of her beautiful Persian carpets that covered our living room from wall to wall, and a set of carpet-like heavy curtains which hung in the door opening between our living and dining rooms until 1945.

Another memory I have of those early years in my life was when, during the winter, my mother and I were sitting by the tile stove in which apples were roasted. She would either teach me some songs or tell me a story, and from time to time we would say a prayer asking God to return my father unharmed from wherever he was working at the time. Before 1933 there was a lot of unemployment and often people would be robbed or even killed. My father always had several young men working for him; some were apprentices, others had become journeymen. They all lived in different villages and all used bicycles to travel.

One story my mother told me when I was older was that I had a very dark-red birthmark on my forehead when I was born, which did not disappear after several months. She had contacted a doctor, who, of course could not help. We lived in the upstairs flat of a house at the time—three rooms, a kitchen and a den—which belonged to a family by the name of Block. They had a very old grandmother living with them about whom all kinds of secretive rumours were told in the village.

This old woman apparently asked my mother one day whether she wanted her baby to be healed of that ugly birthmark. Of course the answer was affirmative and the old woman asked to be alone with the child.

Reluctantly my mother handed me over to her and for about 15 minutes she disappeared with me into her room. When she returned, she said she had "spoken over" the child and the birthmark would soon disappear. Within a few days the mark became lighter and after a month it had completely disappeared.

At this time, while I am writing this, I am 71 years old.[1] Until about a year ago I had never thought about this story again and never noticed anything on my forehead. Recently I can see a faint mark on very cold winter days but I can easily cover it with some make-up. Old "Mutter Blocksch" saved me from later ridicule and superstition; she obviously had powers that no one understood at that time.

•

IN SEPTEMBER, 1928, MY BROTHER Juergen was born, and my mother, who often suffered from severe asthma attacks, needed help. She engaged a 15-year-old girl, Frieda Hinz, to become our nanny. Frieda was the second of four children, had finished school and now needed a job to help her parents, who both were farm hands. Her youngest sister, Brunhilde, or "Hille" as I called her, was two months younger than I, and became my lifelong friend.

I remember very vividly the time of the renovation of the house after my father had bought it from the Block family. I must have been six years old at that time. My mother was very excited to be able to take possession of the whole house and I danced around in the empty rooms. We had a kitchen downstairs now with the luxury of running cold water, and my father had a heating system installed consisting of hot water radiators in each room, upstairs and down. It was heated by an iron stove in the kitchen, with buckets full of pit-coal that had to be lugged up from the dingy basement.

Beside the kitchen and below the upstairs den was the storage room for much of our food. There were lots of shelves with preserves, pots of

---

1   At the final completion of this work, the author was 89.

lard, a bread cutting machine which was turned by hand and cut one slice at a time, and such staples as sacks with sugar, flour, salt, dried goods and so forth. In the summer the table in that room was covered with bowls filled with milk, to be left until the milk soured and turned thick. The top then consisted of a thick cream layer, on which we sprinkled sugar. It made a most delicious dessert.

From the kitchen, you walked into the living room with a red velvet chesterfield, a large round table usually covered with a red velvet tablecloth and two red velvet armchairs, all of which would be valuable antique pieces today. They were an inheritance from my great-grandmother, Oma Bell. In the corner stood our treasured Blaupunkt radio; by the window, my mother's sewing table. A beautiful cherry wood piano, which my father had given to my mother as a gift on the occasion of my birth, completed the furniture. My mother had a beautiful voice and loved to sing. She also played the piano very well, and did so frequently. However, for some reason which I cannot explain to this day, her playing always made me extremely sad, so much so, that I would go into my room, cover my ears and cry my eyes out. This, in turn made my mother very sad, and she began to play less often. Maybe it had something to do with the type of songs she sang and played, such as *The Last Rose* or *The Song Of The Lost Youth*. To these, and certain similar songs, I cannot listen to this day without becoming very emotional and weepy.

On ordinary days we used the living room as a dining room as well, because it was closer to the kitchen. On birthdays, Christmas, Easter and feast days, we ate in the official dining room, located next to the living room. It had a large rectangular table, six chairs, a large china cabinet, and a locked, hand-carved trunk in which special treasures were kept. On a small side table lay the family Bible which was printed in 1754. It measured about 30 by 25 centimetres and was 15 centimetres thick, and had the most beautiful decorative script and pictures. This Bible was an heirloom that had originated in the Hartmann family.

There was also a curio for the china and silverware. Atop the curio stood a mysterious large bulging vase that always intrigued me. One day when I was about 10, my mother took it down to satisfy my curiosity and let me look inside. The bottom was filled with very fine white sand, and on it lay a stack of letters, bundled up with a red ribbon. They were the love letters that my father had written to her before they got married. I was allowed to hold them for a while but not to read them, and never did.

The last room downstairs was my father's office, with his desk and armchair, and shelves full of books and papers.

Upstairs were the bedrooms, one for my parents above the living room; beside it the one for my brother, Juergen, and mine above the office. In each of the bedrooms stood a portable dress closet. None of the houses had built-in closets. Each room also had a washstand: a small table with a large ceramic bowl and matching water pitcher, which always had to be refilled. Under the table stood a pail into which the dirty water was poured, and a chamber pot. On each of our beds lay a thick eiderdown cover, with which we covered ourselves summer and winter. In the winter, however, a down filled so-called "underbed" was added to keep us warm from below as well. As cuddly as it was, it made getting up in the morning into a cold room very unpleasant.

The room above the kitchen was an all-purpose room. It had a linen press, another cold water tap and sink, and the ironing was done there, but mostly my friends and I used it as playroom. When I was ten years old, my father and his friend, Erich Cycelski, built me a dolls' house with about ten rooms in it. My mother furnished it and it was placed permanently in this room, on top of the built-in coal stove which had been covered up. The den beside this room was very small. It only contained a single bed, a chair and a small shelf unit. There was a narrow window, which my brother and I considered the most interesting window in the house. In front of it, in the backyard, stood a large old cherry tree, and the two of us used this window as a platform to climb into the tree to pick the juiciest cherries before they could be harvested and turned into preserves.

The most exciting and mysterious place in the whole house was the attic. It had a high pointed ceiling and covered the complete length and width of the house. It seemed to me that there must have been hundreds of boxes with treasures of all manner and types, old clothes, books, toys, tools and heaven knows what else. Each gable had a big window. Looking toward the south we could see the main part of the village, and above the roofs and trees towered the steeple of our centuries-old church. The south wall of our house was covered with vines of red grapes. In some years they climbed all the way up to the attic window and we had only to reach down to pick the largest and juiciest bunches.

Looking out of the window to the north we could see the train station, the brick factory about two kilometres away, and fields upon fields as far as one can imagine. On clear days we could even distinguish the large forest just south of Stettin, called the *Buchheide* because most of the trees in it were beautiful old beeches.

Close to the center of the attic, on one side, was a small room built around the chimney, which served as a smokehouse. The floor had been covered with bricks and these in turn with beech wood chips. Every year in the fall my father would buy a pig which was killed in the backyard by a few hired men, and each year this was an ordeal for me. I would stay in my room and pull the covers over my ears because I could not stand the screaming of the poor animal.

However, once it was dead, I often watched how it was put into a wooden trough, covered with boiling water and rolled back and forth on chains to get all the hair off. Any remaining hair would be scraped off with a large, metal, bell-shaped tool. One of the women, Frau Hinz, the mother of my friend Brunhilde, always had to stir the blood which ran out of the stabbing wound in the neck. This had to be done by hand to prevent the blood from curdling. I always felt that we were all cannibals, but there was nevertheless this fascination in me to see what went on. The pig was then hoisted on a special ladder and cut open. All the insides were caught in containers, the intestines in a special tub to be turned inside out and cleaned with a hose and again washed several times in salt water. No meat could be used for anything until the meat inspector had come to see whether the pig might have had some parasites in the muscles or organs. After that, it took all day and often the night as well to cut up the meat, grind much of it into sausages, salt the ham, cook the meat, boil the lard and fill all the intestines with the sausage meat.

Back in the smokehouse in our attic was where all ham, bacon and sausages were hung on long sticks over the sawdust and wood chips. These were set afire to smolder for weeks or months, curing and preserving the meat to be eaten in the winter.

The cellar, on the other hand, consisted of three rooms which were all damp and dimly lit by a tiny little window in each room. There was no electric light in the basement and if we had to go down in the evening we either took a flashlight or a burning candle. In the first room we stored the coals for the central heating system. In the fall, my father would order a wagonload of crushed coal, what we called *Koks*, which was dumped in front of the small window through which we shovelled it into the basement, where it formed a big pile and was used up as needed. The same procedure was followed with a wagonload of potatoes, only they were dumped into the second room. The third room contained wooden racks all around the walls which were covered with straw. There were stored the winter supply of apples that we had picked from our own 48 trees.

The buildings on our property were arranged in the shape of a seven. The house faced the front but beside it and to the back was a row of former stables for horses, cows and pigs. The one adjacent to the house had been changed into a "laundry room". It had an enormous built-in kettle in one corner, a cold water tap and sink, and in later years stored our precious wooden washing machine, which featured a swirling wooden cross in the middle that swashed the clothes around. All clothes were boiled before being put in the machine and very soiled ones were rubbed with soap on a metal washboard. After rinsing, they were wrung out by hand, even the largest sheets, and were hung out to dry in the garden, summer and winter. At a later date we acquired a wringer which was attached to the washing machine. It consisted of two rubber rolling pins through which the wet clothes were guided.

This room also served as bathhouse. Each Saturday water would be heated in the big kettle and the family, one after the other, would take a bath in a very large, portable bathtub made of zinc. Usually I was lucky enough to get the first turn, Juergen was next with partly-used water in the tub. I suppose our parents boiled a new kettle of water for themselves. Another use for the kettle was to make lard in it on the day of the pig slaughter. All the fat would be simmered and constantly stirred, with lots of onions, some apples and thyme, until it had become liquid. It then was stored in earthen pots for the winter.

In the fall, there were lots of plums that had to be preserved as plum sauce. They too ended up in the big kettle and with a sackful of sugar and some spices were simmered until they became a thick mass. This procedure sometimes took two days and a night. It had to be stirred constantly to prevent burning at the bottom of the kettle. We always hired someone to do this job for us because it was so exhausting. A special wooden stirrer was used shaped like a seven, the longer part being the handle, and with lots of holes in the shorter part.

Several of the other old barn rooms had been converted into my father's work and storage rooms. Others held garden tools or were empty for us to play in. We always had two or three cats and they also made their home in these buildings. At the very end of this row of buildings was our outhouse, built of wood, insulated with cardboard and decorated with large pictures of cherubs sitting on clouds. It was my assigned job to always cut enough toilet paper in the form of newspaper squares and stick them onto a wire hook beside the "one-seater".

Behind and beside this most important room was the chicken coup. We usually kept about two dozen chickens and a rooster and so always had fresh eggs. Most of the time we owned a dog, too. The one that was by far my favourite was the first one, Myrko. He was a very gentle German Shepherd and my very best friend until I was about five. I remember the heartbreaking day when he had to be put down because he had developed some devastating illness. At the time, of course, I did not know what had happened to him, I just knew that he had died. I believe that my father shot him, because there was no vet far and wide.

Our property was about an acre in size. We had apple trees of different types, several pear trees, plum trees, sweet and sour cherry trees, at least a hundred gooseberry and currant bushes and a large corner of raspberry bushes. Of course, we grew our own vegetables, even some rows of early potatoes. My mother loved gardening and together with the maid that we always had, she transformed part of the garden into a real park area with many flowers, ornamental bushes, a gazebo and natural resting corners with benches and hedges. From her I learned to love gardening and always tried to imitate her ideas.

School Years in the Village

WHEN I WAS SIX YEARS OLD, I entered the village school. The school year always began in the spring after the Easter holidays. Kindergarten classes did not exist; we went straight to Grade 1. We began to learn cursive writing immediately, but it was done on slates with a slate pencil. We all carried this important educational tool in a leather rucksack on our back. The slate was secured in a wooden frame that had a small hole on one side. Through it ran a string to which a damp sponge was attached on one end and a square rag like a pot holder on the other end. The purpose, of course, was to erase our mistakes with the sponge and dry the slate with the rag. Since the slate pencils were quite thin and broke easily, we had to carry several of them in a narrow, polished and decorated wooden box with a sliding top. The pencils themselves were wrapped in coloured paper stamped with designs and pictures to encourage their use.

After about half a year we were asked to bring to school a lined notebook, a wooden penholder and a few nibs as well as an inkwell, and we were taught how to write with ink. It was surprising how fast we learned to become neat writers. My first book had more smears and ink spots in it than letters, which caused me much anxiety, but I always wanted to do well and so I practiced at home every day. In those days, fountain pens, let alone ballpoint pens, had not yet been invented.

The first four years, Grades 1 to 4, were taught by "Herr Frisch". We all attended the same room, as did the Grade 5 to Grade 8 children, who gathered in the second classroom under the tutelage of "Herr Gesch". School hours were from 8 a.m. to 12:30 p.m. with two 10 minute recesses. There was no school in the afternoons. By Grade 3, we had to know our "small" times tables, which are the ones from 2 to 10.

I remember one incident which upset me very much. I was asked how much is 5 times 8, and could not find the answer fast enough. As punishment I had to stay after school and write out the times table and clean out the class closet. In all my school years this was the only time that I was reprimanded by a teacher. It was so traumatic that I always studied until I felt I knew things perfectly.

In Grade 4, we began to study the "large" times tables, from 11 to 20. I also remember that Herr Frisch taught us a lot about local history and the village economy. In a large sandbox, we would build the village with the layout of the fields that belonged to each farmer. We learned what types of crops they planted and why, how they followed an ecological plan by planting grain above the ground one year; in the second year crops that grew below the ground, such as potatoes or sugar beets; the third year the land was plowed but nothing planted and the fourth year alfalfa or a similar plant was sown to enrich the ground again. We also learned that Brietzig was one of very few villages in the area that did not have a "lord" who owned all or most of the land and where everyone else had the status of a serf. The farmers in Brietzig were free, they owned their land, and each one of them had become quite wealthy. [2]

The schoolhouse was a big red brick building which, besides the two classrooms, housed the living quarters of the two families of the teachers. In the schoolyard stood an enormous water pump. Inside the school itself there was no running water, and none of the farm houses had running indoor water either. Plumbing just did not exist and, of course, no one had indoor washroom facilities.

So at the end of the schoolyard, beside the garden of one of the teachers, there was a row of outhouses which we had to use as children.

---

2   Years later, when I took anthropology courses at the University of Toronto, we were taught about the development of agriculture in Europe; about feudalism, free farmers, how properties were inherited and so on. To my surprise, it was precisely what I had learned in my earliest school years, and to a great degree was what I had actually lived through, first-hand.

The largest cubicle at the end was reserved for the teachers and their families.

The school was located at the opposite end of the village from where we lived, up on a hill right beside the very old, walled-in cemetery with the church in the middle. During the 30 Year War (1618-1648), the then-wooden steeple of the church had been burned down. It was thereafter rebuilt as a freestanding stone structure beside the church. In the 18th Century, a talented local miller journeyman by the name of Michael Pahl decorated the inside of our church with wood carvings, many of them hanging from the ceiling. The church had become famous for these inner carvings and stood under the protection of a monument preservation law. It was not unusual for tourists to arrive in buses to see and photograph the church. To this day the church can be visited. [3]

High School

AT THE AGE OF 10 MY PARENTS enrolled me in the *Lyzeum*, which was the high school for girls in the nearby town of Pyritz. From then on and for the next eight years, I would go to school every morning at 7:30 by train and come back at about 3:45 p.m.

It was a funny little train and we all loved it. It ran on a narrow gauge, which was wide enough for a single, small passenger seat on either side of the aisle. Of course it had a huffing and puffing steam engine in front. Following it were usually 10 to 20 freight cars, and at the very end it pulled three or four passenger cars for customers from the seven villages at which it stopped. The names of these villages, starting from Pyritz, were Megow, Brietzig, Kossin, Prillwitz, Kloxin, Rosenfelde and Ploenzig. There, the train would turn around and come back.

The main purpose of this train was to collect all the crops that were

---

3   In 1945, when Pommern (Pommerania) was annexed to Poland, the Lutheran German people having been forced out and catholic Poles moved in, the church took on a catholic character. However, the carvings, the raised pulpit and the moveable alter doors still remain, as does the pipe organ in its original form.

grown in these different communities, for further distribution into the country as a whole. Because there were always lorries to be picked up somewhere, the train was usually late. We did not live far away from the train station and when I heard the train whistle as it crossed a road between Kossin and Brietzig, I got ready and ran in about three minutes to the station.

In all, I only missed it three times. Twice I bicycled the approximately 10 kilometres to school, and once, before the war, my dad took me in his car, but he let me know in no uncertain terms that this would be the one and only time I would be privileged with a ride, and that I had to get up early enough in the future to catch the train.

Due to the fact that the freight cars always had to be maneuvered from one gauge to another and because the train became longer and longer from one village to the next, it happened occasionally that the passenger cars were forgotten. We would sit in them wondering why the train didn't move at all, while the people in Megow would stand at the platform, waiting. When the locomotive driver finally got out to check why nobody got on the train, he came to realize that he first had to return to Brietzig to pick up the forgotten passenger cars.

Of course, as students we loved incidents like this. In winter, it sometimes happened that the train did not even arrive from Pyritz in the morning because of too many high snowdrifts. A crew of snow shovellers first had to clear the tracks, which often enough took half a day and we had a wonderful excuse for having missed a day of school.

There were between two and three dozen students who were regularly picked up in these seven villages each day, and who attended either the *Lyzeum* or the *Gymnasium*, which was the high school for boys. Of course, we all knew each other and were usually quite noisy and behaved like kids and teenagers do. The other passengers didn't like it much if a group of us sat in the same wagon with them, since they were all open from end to end and there was no escape from our noisy chattering. The train conductor finally decided that all students had to use the very last car only, to which we objected and felt discriminated against. However, we were all basically very obedient, and an order was an order. So we confined ourselves to the last wagon, but hung a big sign out of a window in protest, which read: *"Vieh-und Schülerwagen"*—which means Cattle and Student Car.

In 1940, the girls from the *Lyzeum* were all transferred to another, larger building—the so-called *Aufbauschule*; the name indicating that here the lives of the young people would be "built up" to become mature adults. More girls could be accommodated there and a fair number of them could be kept as residential students. [4]

During the second-last year of high school, it was traditional that the students attend an official dance school. Instruction took place once a week in the evening, including such all-important lessons as "how to ask a girl for a dance." (Answer: With a deep bow.) And, "how a girl should accept or reject a dance": (Very politely.) Also, "Who should go up or down the stairs first?" (It always had to be the boy, so that he couldn't look up the girl's skirt going up, and so that if the girl slipped coming down, she would fall on him and break her fall.) Our etiquette lessons also included how to set a table for guests, how to hold a fork and knife and other similar life-enhancing knowledge.

Following these lessons, the actual dances started and at the end of the evening we would walk with our dancing partners around the city on top of the wall or through the Luna Park. We were in love with each other and with life and did not think much about the terrible war that went on not so far away from us.

After three months, the course ended with a gala ball to which the parents were invited as chaperones. It was the only time I ever danced with my father, who did not want to go because he was not a very good dancer. But my mother was adamant that he accompany me, and he finally agreed. I was extremely proud to have him beside me, because he was one of the only fathers who came. On this occasion I wore my first

---

4   In 1943, both the Gymnasium and the Aufbauschule were partly converted to hospitals for wounded soldiers. The girls' school escaped demolition by bombing in 1945, and has become the local hospital in the now Polish city, called Pyriscze. However, the Gymnasium was totally destroyed.

long dress, with silver shoes with high heels. But my father was right about his dancing ability: he had both his heels to the front.

•

AT THE BEGINNING OF 1943, most of the boys my age were drafted to the army. Many girls had left over the years and did not finish high school. Because of the small class enrollments that followed and the lack of space due to the need for hospital rooms, the boys' and girls' classes were combined.

During this last school year, we occupied for several months a room in the City Hall, where on weekends civil wedding ceremonies were performed. Since the workload during the last year was very heavy, and the train ride took a fair amount of time out of the day, my parents felt that I should stay in residence in Pyritz. They made arrangements with their friend, Dr. Fritz Wyczinski, and I moved in with his family. I called his wife "aunt", and got along fine with their two sons, who were a little younger than I.

I graduated with the *Abitur* from Grade 13 in the spring of 1943. There were only two boys left in our class, and eight girls. The final exams were a lot tougher than they are now on this continent. We started writing exams in January of 1943, each week in one subject for three hours. We had to be competent in all subject areas and if we failed one, we had failed them all. There was, of course, the German language essay.

We were given a choice of two topics. One was a description of a personal experience and why it had a special meaning for us. The second choice was the interpretation of a given quote from Goethe, explaining what it meant to us in our own lives and theorizing why the poet might have written it and what it might have meant to him. I chose a saying from Goethe, loosely translated as: "If our eyes were not sun-like, how could we appreciate heavenly joy. If there were no spark of divinity in us, how could we recognize it?"

*Waer' nicht das Auge sonnnhaft, we koennt' uns
Himmlisches entzuecken, laeg' nicht in uns des Gottes
eig'ne Kraft, wie koennt' uns Goettliches begluecken.*

Then there was a dictation and a prescribed text that we had to dissect grammatically, whereafter followed the English essay and dictation, Mathematics, History, Geography, Biology, Chemistry, Physics, Health and Music.

On March 17th, the day of the oral exams arrived. We were all nervous and just lived on adrenalin. The students of the Grade 12 class had prepared a waiting room for us, which was decorated, and displayed several tables filled with all kinds of imaginable treats. At 9 o'clock in the morning, the first of the graduates was called into the examination room. The complete staff was assembled around tables in horseshoe format with a single chair in the middle of the room facing the examiners, which was reserved for one of us poor souls. We had to be prepared in all subjects, because the questions were fired at each of us from all sides and we had no idea in which area we might have to give answers.

Each one of us was examined for about half an hour; my turn came shortly before noon. This was certainly the most stressful day I had experienced so far in my life. I remember getting questioned in History, Biology, English and Physics. By the time I was through and left the room I was in a daze and had no idea how I had done. I was just glad that I had not been examined in mathematics. I silently thanked my mathematics teacher, who knew that I would have been hopelessly lost had he questioned me. The torture of waiting was over and we decided to enjoy the rest of the day by celebrating. As it turned out, all 10 of us had passed the written as well as the oral exams, and at the end of the day, after posing for a group picture taken by a professional photographer, we returned to our more-than-proud parents.

Before the Russian Occupation

THE CITY OF PYRITZ WAS A BEAUTIFUL old town. In the 12th Century it was already "old". It was then that the Bishop, Otto von Bamberg, arrived there and baptized the first Christians.

Pyritz had survived for hundreds of years. In the Middle Ages, a high, thick stonewall had been built surrounding it with a moat encircling the outside. For further protection, a high earthen rampart was formed from the dirt that was shovelled out of the moat. All of these structures were still in excellent condition. The stone wall had been fitted with about ten lookout towers of different sizes and heights, some round, some square, each with its own special name. Four of them had arches for wagons and pedestrians to enter. To the East and West, they were large enough to let pedestrians and small hand wagons get through; in the North and South, horse-drawn wagons and later, cars, could enter. In earlier centuries, these openings all had gates which were closed and locked in the evening, and were manned with guards during the day. The houses within the walls were the oldest, many of them built more than five hundred years ago out of mud bricks and wooden beams, and covered with thatched roofs. These homes were still occupied until their complete destruction in 1945 by Russian soldiers.

The town had been built according to a round plan. You could easily walk around it on the earthen rampart in about 40 minutes. Linden trees grew on both sides all around, and the fragrance of the blooming trees in early summer was absolutely heavenly. Beyond this wall and all around the city, many people had their gardens. On the east side a large park—the Luna Park, with a little creek called the "Knatter" flowing through it—took up several acres. In the south was a small wooded area, and in the West and North, acres of fruit trees of all kinds covered the ground. Each spring, it was such a beautiful sight during the blossom time, that busloads full of tourists from Stettin, Stargard and even from Berlin came to Pyritz to enjoy the sights.

Only beyond this area began the "new town", which in our time had grown considerably in size. Pyritz was known as the "Rothenbury of Pommern"—a beautiful romantic old town, and we teenagers certainly appreciated and loved it.

Brietzig

MY YEARS GROWING UP IN BRIETZIG were carefree and wonderful. Until I was about 14 years old I played a lot with the children from the village. We all spoke in our village dialect. My best friend was Brunhilde Hinz, whom I called Hille. Her sister Frieda, who was 11 years older than we were, had been our "nanny" when my brother Juergen and I were very young, and we had played together from the age of toddlers.[5] I loved Hille and Frieda dearly and do so to this day. Frieda taught us a lot about nature, she made up stories about birds and flowers and gnomes and elves and sun and moon. Due to her influence I came to appreciate the smallest creature and she instilled in me a sense of life's mystery.

Brietzig was built around two main streets which ran in a north-south direction, the "large" and the "small" road. Both were covered with large cobblestones, but had a wide unpaved shoulder that ran beside them for the horse-drawn wagons to use. I remember when the cobblestones were laid—I must have been four or five. The only purpose was for people to avoid getting stuck in the mud on a rainy day. The soil in and around the village was so heavy and loamy that we often lost our boots or shoes in wet areas if we didn't watch out. This type of soil made the earth very fertile and the area was widely known as *Weizackerland*, meaning wheatfield land.

At both ends of the village the two streets met, our house being close to the northern end and to the railroad. The school, the church and the cemetery were located at the southern end, where the village ended at the foot of the *Wartberg*, the highest elevation far and wide. The transla-

---

5   Frieda died on New Year's Day, 2011 in Lübeck, at the age of 96, having lived the last six years of her life in a wheelchair.

tion would be "Waiting Mountain". It had received its name
ries ago, when Christianity was first brought to the area by
von Bamberg who had entered Brietzig prior to arriving in
people had climbed up onto this high hill to await his coming. Halfway
up on this mountain grew a little grove of fir trees which was my very
favourite place to visit. More often than not I did my homework there,
or just went there to read. Later, I met with my boyfriend Dieter in this
spot, and lots of times my friend Hille and I discussed our dreams, hopes
and wishes for the future there.

Until I was about 10 or 11 years old, a windmill stood a little higher
up and to the west of this fir grove. It was in daily use, especially before my father connected electricity to the mill in the village. One summer night in 1936, the old windmill was struck by lightning and burned
down, and though it was a sad loss to tradition, it brought the farmers
another step closer to modernization. Emil Naumann, the miller, was
now busier than ever. He owned the mill in the village, updated it and
my father put in the electricity to get the modern machines running.
Emil was also the cousin of my mother and we often had occasion to go
there. I loved the smell in the mill and though we were always warned
of the dangers in the building, we still used it as hiding place and part of
our playground, just minding to stay out of the way of the miller or the
farmers.

Every 24th of June the people would start a large bonfire in the evening at the highest point of the *Wartberg* to celebrate the longest day of
the year—a leftover of a former pagan ritual. We would all stand around
the fire, watching it light up the night. When it was burned down low,
young couples would take a run at it and jump over to assure a happy
future together.

As a child, I liked winter even more than summer. Each year brought
mountains of snow, through which we could build tunnels and castles.
We had two favorite places to go sleigh riding: the "millerhill" and the
Wartberg. For my 16th birthday I received a pair of skis, which made
me the envy of the other kids. I soon learned how to use them and that
winter and the next I spent on the *Wartberg* skiing downhill. In the fol-

lowing year, however, people were asked to donate what they could to the German army in Russia, and I sacrificed my beloved skis, never in all my life to ski again.

Since we did not have a pond in the village, none of us ever learned how to skate. There were a few small lakes about four or five kilometres north of the village and once, Dieter, my first boyfriend, another girl and I ventured there with borrowed skates to try our luck. However, the other girl broke her foot and we had to carry her all the way home, which was no easy task. This was the beginning and end of my skating experience.

People in the village liked children and we had the whole community to use as our playground. Nobody minded if a group of us suddenly appeared in their yard or garden or stables or even in their houses to play hide and seek, which was one of our favorite pastimes. One of these games we called *Oberland und Unterland* or *Schnitzeljagd*, which meant "land above and land below" and "paper chase". We would divide into two groups, 10 to 15 children in each group. One group would go and hide anywhere in the village, sprinkling sawdust from a bag as they went, trying to mislead the search group as much as possible by creating false tracks. During these games I became very familiar with the households and barnyards of the farmers. We would hide in the most impossible places, in haylofts, in barns, in the mill, in attics or in dingy basements. Once, I remember, we climbed into the church belfry and watched the search party from above, combing the area until we became bored after a few hours and descended to start all over again.

Another favorite game for the girls was playing ball against the wall. We did this for hours on end and never got tired of it. To this day I love to play it and do it sometimes with my grandchildren, Jessica and Conrad. But because it requires a great amount of skill they can't keep up with me and give up after a while. I wish they would practice as we did, hitting a medium-sized soft ball, preferably one with many colours, with our forehead against the wall, 20 times; then with folded hands 19 times, with a fist 18 times, with one arm 17 times and so on, until by the count of one, all body parts had been used and several in combination more than once. I remember that number one was always to hit head, chest, arm, knee, then head, chest and arm a second time, all without dropping the ball. I became so good at this game that I could do this last contortion many times over without stopping and without ever dropping the ball.

Every free minute I had in the winter I would take my sled (we did not know toboggans) and go to the *Muellerberg*—the hill beside the mill, which started at the schoolhouse—and slide down that hill like dozens of other children until hunger drove us home. It truly was a wonderful time to grow up in that little village.

·

THERE WERE SOME UNIQUE peculiarities to the farmhouses in Brietzig. Most of them were built in the Tudor style with the front gable facing the street. The entrance door was in the middle with one or two windows on either side. You entered into a very long hall, from which doors to the left and right led into a parlour, bedrooms and a general family room.

At the end of the hall you arrived in the kitchen. Each had brick floors, that were swept daily with a straw broom after very fine white sand had been strewn all over. The kitchen had enormous coal stoves made out of iron, and the fire was never extinguished. When clothes had to be ironed, the hollow iron was filled with hot coal from the stove. Meals were usually eaten at a long wooden table in the kitchen or in a room adjacent to it, which served as food storage room at the same time.

Beyond the kitchen you found the laundry room. It too had a brick floor. In one corner stood a huge, built-in kettle, in which the clothes were boiled on each washday. That happened usually once every two weeks. It was an enormous job and the washday started at 5 a.m. because the clothes had to hang on the line by 9 a.m. for everyone to see. Hanging them up at a later time indicated to the rest of the women in the village that the woman of that house was lazy. The same kettle was used to cook plum jam and to make lard and sausages, just as we did at our house.

Behind this laundry room was the barn, still all under the same roof in the same long stretched building. The first room was the fodder room, in which large bins with all kinds of grains and dried animal foods were stored and mixed before use. It also contained a huge step-on scale with iron weights, wooden and metal pails as well as the large cans in which the milk was collected to be transported to the local milk-and-cheese factory. In the first part of the actual barn were the horses, because they were the least smelly animals, followed by the cows. If the farmer had some sheep—most did not—they were next and at the very end of the building the pigs were housed.

The whole length of the houses were covered with a straw roof. Brietzig had about a dozen of these old houses and they all had been declared to be "national treasures". [6]

This manner of building houses had been done for hundreds of years and, of course, had the advantage that the farmer did not have to go outside in the winter to feed the animals. The main reason, however, had been that the presence of the animals kept the main house warmer in the winter. There was no such thing as central heating. Each room had its own tile stove which used up a lot of firewood and coal, so in the winter usually only the kitchen was warm, and at Christmas time the parlour or salon was heated. I know all these details because my friends were all farmers' daughters and I went in and out of their houses regularly.

Another interesting feature of the area was the little creek, which we called *Fliess*, meaning flowing water, that wound through part of the village. It was one of our favourite play areas. The water was clear and shallow with many pebbles and little stones in the creek bed.

When we played anywhere, we hardly ever wore shoes. Usually we ran around in wooden slippers, which could quickly be thrown off and picked up, leaving us to run fast or wade in the creek. In winter they were absolutely perfect for sliding on ice or snow.

In the *Fliess* were a number of large rocks, on which the women used

6   At my first visit after the Second World War, in 1981, only one of these houses remained, and it was in poor repair. The others had all been replaced by ugly cement block houses.

to wash the potato and grain sacks. They used homemade soap and hit the wet sacks on the rocks with a wooden flail. After rinsing, they were spread out to dry on the rocks. Beside the *Fliess* grew many old lilac bushes. We children had shaped them in such a way that they served us either as hiding places or to play "house" in them. We brought our dolls and toys there and often left them for days, always to find them exactly as we had left them several nights before.

During the fall months, my friend Hille always had the job of watching her parents' flock of geese, about two dozen of them. I often accompanied her into the stubble fields which were left after the grains had been cut. I remember that even there, we did not wear shoes or even the wooden slippers, but ran barefoot after the geese if they wandered off too far. We always took a picnic lunch which consisted of rye bread sandwiches, cut from a 10-pound loaf, with either lard or plum jam or both, and a bottle of water mixed with vinegar and sugar. We also knew which plants were edible and which were not, because we tried them all and so we supplemented our feast with berries and seeds from various "weeds".

Both of us liked the barns. We often mucked out the cow barn behind her parents' house, pretending that one of the cows might turn into a prince and be very grateful that we had kept his barn clean. We also liked to mash the boiled potatoes in a large trough for the pigs, mixing them with hot water and some grains into a real mush, and then watch the pigs and piglets gobble it down.

In the summer months my mother often would take a group of us children to the nearby brick factory, whose owner we knew, of course, like everyone else in the village. It was a walk of about one kilometre that brought us to the loam quarry from which the brick material was gathered. Over the years it had become quite deep and was partly filled with ground water up to about four feet. It was always a special treat when we went there, because we were not allowed to go alone, without an adult. It was the only nearby "lake" that we could go swimming in and it could be potentially dangerous. We mainly just splashed around and hunted for frogs and pollywogs that lived there by the thousands. In the steep walls of the quarry hundreds of swallows had dug their nests in the soft soil and we often saw rabbits and foxes. While we amused ourselves, my mother would pick several containers full of brambleberries that grew in profusion around the edges. At home they would be mashed, then dumped into a cheesecloth that was tied to the four legs of an upside-down chair on the table and left until the last bit of juice had drained out into a catch basin. With this method we preserved all kinds of juices for the winter.

Another well-liked hiking trail for us was in the *Heidberge*. This was a large forest area, about three or four kilometres south of Brietzig, very hilly and very sandy. Only pine trees and heather grew there and on the highest point stood a wooden tower, which we loved to climb. I always felt somewhat awed by this forest; it seemed mysterious and full of un-knowns. It was a most quiet place, far from human activity and I loved to lie on my back among the heather, staring at the passing clouds and listening to the humming of the bees, the chirping of the crickets and the singing of the birds.

In the opposite direction, to the northeast of the village lay another forest, surrounding the *Ploenesee* (Lake Ploene), about seven or eight ki-lometres from the village. This was a mixed forest with all kinds of deer and elk. As we got older, we were allowed to ride there on our bikes and go swimming. A narrow walking path led from the road through high grasses to the water which was shallow and not dangerous, except that you could end up with some leeches on your legs.

Usually we did not venture too far into the forest for fear that we might encounter an elk or even a wild boar. But one Sunday, when we were a larger group, we went exploring and came upon an old hunters' lookout stand. Juergen, my brother, was about 11 at the time and he de-cided to climb up to get a better view of the land. When he reached the highest rung on the ladder, he screamed suddenly and climbed down, falling more than climbing. One of the rungs broke and he did fall the last metre or two. He had disturbed a hornets' nest on top of the lookout and had been stung in his face and a few times on his arm. In no time at all his face swelled up and he cried in anguish. We left our bikes and stumbled through the thicket, yelling for help. By good luck we came upon the forester's house not long after, and because it was an isolated house, he had a telephone. We called home and my father came to pick up Juergen with his car, which we had by then, and took him to the nearest doctor. He had to stay in bed for about a week and was lucky that help had been available so soon. It could have been a sad ending. After that adventure we never went through that forest again.

Another mishap that caught up with Juergen at about the same age occurred during the winter when he rode down the *Wartberg* on his sled, lying on his stomach. He landed, head first, against a tree at the bottom of the hill. I had seen it happen and ran toward him, seeing that he was unconscious and bleeding. Some other children helped me to put him back on the sled and then we ran as fast as we could home, dragging him behind us. Again the doctor had to be summoned and several days of house arrest followed.

Family Traditions

OUR BIRTHDAYS WERE ALWAYS very special events. When my brother and I were very young, we were allowed to invite all our friends from the village, sometimes up to twenty children. The highlight at Juergen's birthday every September was an evening procession through part of the village and our large garden with lit Chinese lanterns. If there were more children than lanterns they would carry willow branches, bent into horseshoe shape, decorated from end to end with coloured paper roses that we had fashioned ahead of time. Since my own birthday fell in winter, my processions could at best march through the house.

As a special treat we watched what was called *Laterna Magica.* It was a kind of slide projection, at which the pictures, mainly cartoon characters, were painted on a long glass pane which was then fed through an extremely simple projector and reflected onto a large white sheet. To us this was a most exciting treat, since we had never seen photo slides, let alone a movie, and nobody had ever heard of television. Even photographs in the 1920s and '30s could only be produced in black and white and these pictures on our wall were in colour! What a miracle!

The tradition of our Christmas celebration was quite different from the one we came to know later in life after we immigrated to Canada. It began on December 1st, when each of the children received what we called an "Advent Calendar". I remember a large golden star with 24 small, numbered cutout stars on it. Each day we took one small star out and found behind it on a red background a little picture and a number. It told us, how many more days we had to wait until Christmas Eve. On the 24th of December, we knew there would be the picture of the nativity behind the star in the middle. In later years, the star was replaced with calendars of various Christmas themes and now, at the end of the 20th Century, this German custom has been brought to North America. However, now the children find behind each little door, in addition to the picture, a piece of chocolate and a little Christmas verse.

Each of us children back then knew that December 6th was St. Nicholas day. This meant that on the evening of December 5th, and from then on every evening until the 24th, we would put our shoe on the window sill before going to bed, because St. Nicholas came by every night to deposit a treat in the shoes of those children who had been good. However, whoever had been naughty, disobedient or lazy in school, would find a *Rute* in his or her shoe. This was a bundle of willow branches tied up at one end, and St. Nicholas expected the parents to give that child a spanking with it.

Decorated Christmas trees were nowhere to be seen in the village until the 24th, in the evening. The farmers always set up their trees a few days before in the parlour and then locked the door. In our house, the tree stood in the dining room, which had one door leading into the hall and one opening covered with a heavy curtain leading into the living room. For about three or four days before Christmas the door to the hall was locked, as was the door from the kitchen to the living room. Meals were eaten in the living room, but only with the parents present, and my brother and I didn't dare to peek through the curtain.

We were, however, allowed to peek through the keyhole in the hall door, and once in a while we would hear a noise inside and glimpse a shimmer of light or the reflection of a shining ornament, which built great suspense.

All through December the house smelled of baked goods, spices and baked apples. Throughout the day of December 24th at any odd time, little wrapped presents would suddenly fly through the house, accompanied by a deep voice shouting *Yulklapp*. "Yul", of course, meaning yuletide and "klapp" meaning a clapping noise. The tension and excitement would rise from hour to hour, when around 4 p.m. we got dressed up to go to church for the Christmas service at six. Naturally we walked through the village up the hill to the church. It was always filled to the very last seat and there, for the first time, we would in awe behold a large, beautiful Christmas tree, decorated with silver tinsel and lit by many open flame candles.

Everyone in the village, including our family, was Lutheran. Not until many years later in history class did I hear for the first time, that other people had other denominations and that something called "the Catholic Church" even existed.

Our minister, Pastor Pfeiffer, would read the Christmas story and the congregation would sing all the beautiful old German Christmas hymns, with teacher Gesch playing the organ and teenagers moving the air bellows by stepping on them. On our way home we could glimpse here and there a lit Christmas tree through some windows. People were not accustomed to decorating the outsides of their houses. For many years every tree was lit by wax candles; I remember how careful we had to be around the tree. Over the years, when my father had laid electric wires into the houses, more and more electric tree lights were used, our house being the first one.

After we arrived home from church, the evening meal was served. It was always very simple: potato salad and Vienna wieners. This custom probably developed out of necessity because of the prevailing excitement and impatience. After all dishes were cleared away with the help of everyone, finally, the great moment arrived: in the Christmas room a bell would ring. Our father, who had been the Christchild's helper—for the Christchild would bring the gifts and the *Weihnachtsmann* (Santa Claus) only carried the sack for Him—would pull the heavy curtain to the side very slowly and there stood in all its glory the lit Christmas tree with tinsel and shining ornaments and lots of chocolate and jelly rings on it.

This moment for me was always so overwhelming that it took my breath away. It took a while to take in all the grandeur. There was an enormous sack beside the tree filled with wrapped parcels and under the tree lay more presents. The celebration began with both Juergen and me, in turn, reciting a Christmas poem in front of the tree. This was followed by singing a few songs, to which our mother accompanied us on the piano and sometimes our dad played the violin. Only then did we each gingerly pick a present out of the sack, open the ribbon without cutting it and the paper without tearing it. Everyone waited to see what each package contained; there was never any rushing or squabbling. On the contrary, we all tried to prolong these wonderful surprises as much as possible. In the end, all the treasures were spread out under the tree and remained there until at least the New Year, being admired and played with daily.

Until the 6th of January we were each allowed to eat one chocolate ring daily from the tree. On that day, all of us took the tree down and we divided the rest of the candies. Many years later, when we came to Canada, we brought our customs with us and for many years, as long as our children, Garrett and Roland, were young and living at home, we celebrated as much as possible in the same way.

CHAPTER TWO

War Years as a Teenager

W hen the war broke out in 1939 I was 14 years old and began to associate more with my school friends from Pyritz rather than with the children from the village, and often invited some of them to my parents' house. My mother encouraged these visits because she always wanted to know who my friends were. She had a very beautiful way of getting along with young people. All my friends loved her and those with whom I have kept in contact talk about her even now, at the end of the century, and remember how kind she had always been to them.

My mother was very good at writing poetry and many of her poems still exist in German. She had written about the village, the people in it, and for and about special events. For the birthdays of my brother and me, she would write little songs about us and our guests, invent games and motivate us to become inventive ourselves.

Once or twice each year she would organize a Sunday afternoon or an evening for the parents, at which all the children from the village would participate in songs, poems, skits or dances. For weeks prior to this she would practice with us in the dance hall of the village inn, called *Gasthof Braun*, which had the only stage in the village. On the day of the performance the hall was always packed to overflowing, which made us feel very important. It also made the parents happy, as well as Gastwirt Braun, who sold a lot of beer afterwards. Everyone in the village liked my mother very much. My father was also very well liked; he was not only a very kind man but was so very important to the modernized functioning of all the farms.

At the end of August 1939, my father was drafted. I remember very well that we accompanied him to Stettin, where he had to report. My brother and I did not realize what terrible times lay ahead, but my mother was in tears and I had an uncomfortable feeling of foreboding. Both our parents, of course, remembered the First World War in which my father had been an active soldier on the Eastern Front, but there was absolutely nothing that anyone of us could do at this point.

We did not see our father again for the next two years. He became, like all soldiers at the time, attached to the army that invaded Poland in September of that year. Since he was a specialist, he was lucky to be ordered to stay behind the fighting lines. It was his duty to re-erect the electrical wires that had been torn down by the fighting troops, or that were damaged for any other reason. Through letters, which we received later from him, we found out that it had been just a matter of days before he had become seriously ill. I personally think that it probably had something to do with the horrible things he must have seen. We were informed that he had been transported to the west of Germany into a hospital in Trier at the river Mosel, with bleeding ulcers. He never really recuperated from his illness and for that reason was not redrafted. In 1942, he was discharged from the military and sent home to Brietzig.

Nevertheless, everybody was obliged to perform some duty for his country, and he was requested to relocate to Lissa, a town of about 30,000 people in the former *Warthegau*, which had belonged to Poland between 1918 and 1939, not far from Posen. Both cities are now Polish again, since 1945. He was assigned to reestablish all electricity in the town and at the same time he ran a store which sold electrical equipment and appliances, and which was mainly looked after by a young Polish girl named Wanda. I remember that the address of the store was Adolf-Hitler Str. 22. Our father, whom we called *Vati*, rented a "room and board" with two old German ladies, who owned a house in Lissa. This meant, of course, that he was away from our home in Brietzig most of the time. He came home by train every few months for a few days and then had to leave again.

During the summer of 1942, all 17-year-old girls had to perform some duty to help out in the war economy. We had several options: farm work, streetcar conductor in a larger city, or hospital work. I opted for the latter and applied for a position in a clinic in Posen that dealt specifically with premature babies and orphans under two years of age. My father had finalized the arrangement and for three months I lived with my cousins Heinz and Erika Gerlach in Posen. They had two little girls, four and two years old, and I felt very much at home with them.

Every morning I would go by public transportation to this hospital to help the nurses with the care of the very young children. I learned a great deal about baby care, which came in very handy years later when I had my own two babies.

Since Lissa wasn't that far from Posen, I had the opportunity to visit my father from time to time, especially on the weekends. Sometimes I would visit him, sometimes he would come to Posen and visit me. I liked very much to be in his store and help Wanda, with whom I became quite friendly. During these months my dad and I became very close. I was proud when he showed me how to repair small appliances, such as an iron for instance, and I loved it when he took me to a movie. I still think of him as one of the handsomest men I ever saw and I knew that I was very special to him too. I tried to live up to all his expectations and wanted him to be proud of me.

Then finally in 1943 my school years were over.

During this last year my mother had arranged for two very memorable parties for me. The first one took place late in the summer of 1942 in our backyard. I had invited my school friends, boys and girls, who arrived with me by train after school and we had a most wonderful teenager party that lasted all through the night with dancing and singing and feeling grown up. Though my mother stayed discretely away from our party, I doubt that she found any sleep at all that night.

The next morning, the train took us back to school, overtired, but with a feeling of wickedness. At that time I did not have a particular boyfriend, having stopped seeing my first love, Dieter Fewson, who had become boring to me. We had met when we were both 15, when he stayed with a family in Brietzig while his parents lived elsewhere. We sat together on the train going to school; sometimes we walked through the fields or rode our bikes. The most secret thing I ever did was telling my mother on Juergen's birthday, that I was going to visit Hille Pfeiffer to do some homework but instead rode with Dieter into the *Heidberge* where we climbed the wooden tower and talked.

One late evening in the summer, he and his friend Peter sneaked into our garden and hoisted every bench, table and chair they could find into the various trees. The next morning my mother and I laughed, but my father and a few of his men had to take time out to lift all the garden furniture down again.

During the winter months of 1941-42, before all the boys were drafted into the army, we had all enrolled in the traditional dance club lessons. We learned all the ballroom dances and got etiquette lessons thrown in with the deal. At that time I still liked Dieter Fewson and he was my dancing partner. My dad did not particularly like him—maybe he would not have liked any other boy to go out with me either, but my mother always put in a good word for me and I was allowed the odd time to stay overnight in Pyritz with a family my father knew. This way I was able to go to a movie or just hang out with my friends. But by the spring of 1942 this friendship with Dieter ended.

The second big party at our house took place in March 1943, after the *Abitur*—the Grade 13 exam. I had found a new boyfriend, whom I really liked. He was the son of the minister in the neighbouring village of Kloxin and we met daily on the train. With him I attended several operettas in Pyritz, often went to movies with him, but mostly we took walks around the city along the mote wall. At that time my parents had acquired a telephone and Hans-Ulrich and I made good use of this new invention.

At this second party we were about seven or eight couples. Again we celebrated all through the night, but my mother and brother, of course, were there too, while my father still lived in Lissa. Each room in the house had been transformed into a theme room. There was a Japanese tearoom, a gambling casino, a restaurant, a ballroom, an Hawaiian beach hut and a lounge. The memory of this party is one of the fondest of my young years; it's no wonder all my friends adored my mother for making all this possible for us.

I stayed in contact with Hans-Ulrich for several years. He, too, was drafted and after the war he ended up in East Germany, which was the last place on earth I wished to go back to. He became a Lutheran minister, married, had one daughter and when we were both 65 years old, after the fall of the Berlin Wall and the reunification of West and part of East Germany, we met again. I invited him and his wife for a visit to Canada and they spent a few weeks during the summer of 1995 with me in Mississauga. He hasn't changed much; however, I am glad that I did not have to share his life in East Germany with him, but was instead privileged to live in freedom in Canada. What ever happened to Dieter Fewson, nobody seems to know. [1]

Reichsarbeitsdienst: RAD

HAVING PASSED THE ABITUR examination on March 17, 1943, I had a few weeks off. A draft letter had arrived, which informed me that on April 24th I had to report to the so-called RAD, short for *Reichsarbeitsdienst*, a national labour duty to which all girls at about that age were called. What it meant was that we had to perform a service for the country, free of charge.

Again there was a choice: either we could become train or streetcar conductors, help out in a hospital or go into the country and help out on farms. Most girls were needed in the latter position. At that time many of the cities had been bombed already and I had no death wish. So I reported to the assigned camp not far from the town of Demmin, west of the river Oder in Vorpommern.

---

[1]   I later learned he survived the war, married and lives near Stuttgart.

I had been sent a list of the things I would need and was to bring. It was very short: underwear, toothbrush, soap, writing paper and a sewing kit—absolutely no luxury items. On my arrival in Demmin I noticed that there were at least a dozen other girls who seemed to have the same destination as I did. As we looked around we saw two young women in greenish-brown uniforms with a hat of the same colour and a white blouse. They were standing beside a horse drawn wagon that had benches placed lengthwise in the back. They realized, of course, that we were the ones they were looking for. They introduced themselves as two of the six or seven leaders of the camp Tenzerow. Having seated us all on the wagon, they drove us for another eight or 10 miles to the actual camp, where we were to stay for the following six months.

I had been away from home a few times before but never for such a long time. My first time alone away from home had been when I was nine years old. My mother had to have a gall bladder operation, which at that time was still a matter of life and death. So my father took me to his oldest sister, my aunt Else in Berlin and my brother to his younger sister Gertrud, who was married and lived in Konstadt in Oberschlesien, very close to the Polish border. I was sent to school in Berlin and stayed with Tante Else for about half a year. Another time, when I was twelve, I was sent to a childrens' recuperation home in the Harz mountains for about eight weeks, after having barely survived diphtheria, and the following year I had visited a family we knew in the Thuringia Forest in Sonneberg. Each time I had had a bit of homesickness, but I had always been treated as a guest.

In Tenzerow, the situation was quite the reverse and for the first six weeks I had a serious bout of homesickness, knowing there was absolutely no way to escape. It had a lot to do with the rigorous schedule we had to follow.

At 5:30 in the morning the day began. At the sound of a loud whistle we had to jump out of bed and get into a jogging suit and running shoes which had been provided for each of us. At a second whistle three minutes later we lined up outside for a 20-minute morning run. Returning from it, we proceeded down to the basement into a large room which contained at least two dozen shower heads that spouted cold water on us. Warm water was just not available. Our official title was *Arbeitsmaiden*, or work maids, and there were 84 of us in this camp. We would all jump shivering and screaming, stark naked under the cold water and supervision of one of the leaders, who made sure that nobody skipped this cleansing ritual.

Being fully awake now, we returned to our rooms to make our beds, which had to be done according to specific rules. Another whistle let us know that it was morning inspection time. This meant, each bed and each locker, beside which we had to silently wait, would be inspected. At the beginning, many beds were pulled apart again and had to be done over and over until not a single crease was visible. I occupied an upper bunk bed in the largest room which housed 20 girls and was dubbed "The Zoo". The other rooms were a little smaller with 10 to 16 beds in each, all of them bunk beds, wooden boards covered with straw, which in turn was covered with a sheet and blankets. The pillow, too, was stuffed with straw.

Each of the six or seven leaders had their own small room on the main floor. The building in which we were housed had once been a beautiful old mansion and had been privately owned. It was a three story, white house with numerous large and small rooms with balconies, and a huge kitchen. Surrounding it lay a very large park-like garden with a sizeable pond, wide grassy areas, high trees and a vegetable garden. In front of the main entrance were wide steps leading from a circular driveway onto a terrace. In the middle of this driveway stood the flagpole.

Once the aforementioned inspection was over and we were all dressed in our work clothes—except for Sundays, when we wore our greenish-brown uniform suits—yet another whistle called us to stand at attention in the rounded driveway around the flagpole and watch solemnly as two girls would hoist up the flag. One of the leaders would then recite either a nationalistic poem or a thought for the day, following which we would sing one of the then-approved songs, answer to the roll call and then march into the huge dining hall—which once upon a time must have been a beautiful ballroom—for breakfast. The food we were served was another reason for my initial homesickness. Neither I nor the other girls were accustomed to the porridges in the morning and the stew-like dinners we were served. However, we all became used to it, especially since there were absolutely no snacks available and we were always hungry. After breakfast each morning between 7:30 and 8:30, there was an hour of singing. This was my favourite time of the day. I learned many beautiful folk songs that year and loved to hear us sing as a big choir in three- and four-part harmony.

Our leader in charge divided us each Monday morning into small groups with different responsibilities. Some had to do kitchen duty, others worked in the washhouse, which nobody liked, still others tended the garden or had house cleaning duties. However, most of us were sent out to various farms from which the men had been drafted into the army and where the women needed help. Though the "home duties" changed every week, the farm assignments lasted at least six weeks. I considered myself lucky to have always been assigned to a farm, although some of the places where I ended up were not very pleasant. I remember one house that was terribly dirty and the woman seemed to be unable to talk without screaming. I felt rather intimidated at first but had enough insight to realize that she did not know any better so I tried my best to please her.

The best placement was one in a bakery. It was a fair distance away, but we all had bicycles to get to our assigned families. The woman had help from her father and a Polish prisoner of war, and there was always a coffee break with lots of bread to eat. I remember that on the way back another girl and I had to drive along a cherry tree flanked road. At that time the cherries were ripe and we would stop and climb a tree, stuffing our pockets and mouths full of cherries, and then ride at high speed to be back at camp in time.

Six o'clock was dinner time, followed by scheduled evening activities. They were either poetry reading or story reading (one person reading aloud to the whole group), or we mended our socks or wrote letters, or did arts and crafts or rehearsed plays, which we then performed on some Sunday afternoon, or we took an evening walk through the fields or the nearby forest, always with one of our young leaders present. Even our Sundays were scheduled, although we had two or three hours of free time. We were not allowed to leave the camp grounds; we were free only to decide whether we wanted to read or write or talk or sleep and whether we wanted to sit inside or in the garden. Though we detested the rigorous schedules, we all learned a great deal of self-discipline, punctuality and we all became very duty-bound. Most of all, it taught us to stick together. There was a tremendous sense of comradeship among us, especially because we were quite cut off from the outside world.

Our work clothes consisted of a blue linen dress with a wide skirt and puffed sleeves, a red half apron and a red kerchief which we always had to tie around our head. Only once were we allowed to wear civilian clothes to attend a show. Only once were we allowed to receive a visitor from home. Not many parents came, but my mother was there!

Only once were we able to visit home for a weekend and this only applied to those of us who could make the train trip in one day. I remember leaving on a Saturday, being home on Sunday and returning on Monday. I remember the elated feeling I had when I finally sat in that little train that took me from Pyritz to Brietzig. When I saw my mother at the train station it was just like coming home to paradise.

The train station really was nothing more than a corrugated tin hut, and everybody referred to it as "the hut". Outside on either end was a bench, consisting of a tree cut in half lengthwise, while inside the floor was covered with bricks and a bench that ran around three sides. The fourth side was sectioned off to house the local train conductor, who sold tickets through a sliding window. That evening my mother sent me to the store to buy something and I remember, on the way back, losing the change I had gotten—three dimes and a nickel. It was dark, but I went back to the spot where I thought I might have lost it and felt with both hands over the ground, and sure enough, I found each piece. I remember this incident so well because even at that time it made me understand how connected I was to this place, to the earth and how well I knew every little bump in the dirt road to the extent of finding a needle in a haystack.

For all the work we did at the camp we received six German Marks per month. With that, we bought toothpaste, shampoo, stamps and postcards. Other than these few items, we really didn't need anything. By the time the harvest had been brought in, our time in Tenzerow came to an end; we were no longer needed. By this time I had made many good friends, especially one, called Annemie. [2]

First Teaching Experience

ALL OF US WERE OBLIGED TO OFFER our time and services for a whole year in some capacity and the year was only half over. This time we were given no choice. We were all sent to an underground ammunition factory in Barth, a small town near Stralsund by the Baltic Sea.

Before we left Tenzerow I was, to my utter surprise, promoted to *Kameradschaftsaelteste*, which means I now was the "Elder" in charge of a group of 12 other girls. I had never thought of myself as a leader, but it was a thrilling feeling to think that people in authority thought me capable of becoming one. I promised myself to do my darn best to be good at it—and I was. The other girls liked me, I never bossed anyone but always was very polite to each one, as my mother had taught me to be. We felt that our group, among the hundreds of others, was very special and functioned like a real family unit. We shared our duties and privileges and went together on outings during our rare days off.

We were housed in stone barracks that were built in the middle of a forest. Above them and above the roads, nets were hanging from tree to tree, covered with branches to camouflage the whole area. Our actual workplace was underground, which we would reach by elevator. There

---

2   Annemie came to visit me many years later, in the 1970s when I lived in Toronto. She had changed. It was an interesting and challenging visit as Annemie turned out to be a lesbian, and we had to sleep in the same bed. I refused her advances and she got so mad at me she slept in the backyard, which was about the only other place to go. Annemie also had a fondness for alcohol, which in the end contributed to her death in her early 40s.

we all stood by conveyor belts, filling small metal containers with powder and putting on lids. We were never told what kind of powder it was, but we wore gloves and no one was allowed to smoke. Aside from us girls, who still had to wear our uniform each day, there worked in this factory hundreds of civilian people, mainly women, who all lived in the surrounding villages. We all ate in shifts in an enormous hall. The food was good, but we hated our work.

A few weeks before Christmas I was called into an office and was told that I had been reassigned. Since I had finished a high school education, I was to take over the position of a teacher in the small town of Triebsees, where teachers were desperately needed. I had to leave immediately. By now, leaving my friends behind was almost as hard as leaving home all over again. The only bright spot was that I got away from this awful gunpowder factory and for that, all the others envied me.

The following day I reported to the leader in the RAD camp in Triebsees. This camp was not nearly as nice and comfortable as the one in Tenzerow. Whereas we had lived in this beautiful old stone mansion, I now found myself in one of many wooden barracks that had not been winterized. Thankfully I was assigned to a small room near the entrance, which I was to share with another girl who arrived the same day as I did, and who also had her *Abitur*.

Both of us reported the following day to the principal of the local public school, who assigned our classes to us. I was given a Grade 2 class with 45 girls to teach in the morning, and a Grade 5 afternoon class of 56 boys. The principal was the only man on staff. Neither he nor any of the other female teachers offered us any help, advice or direction at any time. I can't even remember what the staff room looked like; I was in it not more than once or twice briefly.

The two of us felt very isolated and after awhile all our initial enthusiasm began to fade. We were left completely to our own ingenuity, checked what kinds of books we could find and otherwise relied on our memory of our own school years, trying to imitate the teachers we had had in our younger years. In the afternoons after school, we worked hard to prepare for the next day, but it was all in a haphazard way. We tried our best and under the circumstances I think we did a very good job.

Keeping discipline was, of course, the hardest task. Thankfully, children in those years were still much more obedient than they are now and punishments such as standing in the corner or staying after school were still quite acceptable. We both were grateful that we did not have to participate in the regular camp activities, except to attend the morning role call and the mealtimes. All in all, neither one of us liked these months very much; they were filled with stress and uncertainty and we counted the days until the end of the school year, which always took place around Easter.

One incident I remember was the visit of a mouse in our room for several nights. This made me so nervous and upset that I did not get any sleep at all. I was always trying to chase the little beast and it never went out the door. One night it climbed on the windowsill and I pinned it down with the curtain, but after holding it there for about 10 minutes I had to let it go again and lo and behold, it disappeared. We didn't hear or see it again until the last day in camp, when we had handed in our uniforms and got out our one and only civilian dress. There was the mouse, dried out, entangled in the sleeve of my dress, which was completely torn to shreds. I cut it off and wore it home with one sleeve. I was grateful to have a jacket to wear over it.

In the spring of 1944 I arrived again, home, in Brietzig.

CHAPTER THREE

Life as an Apprentice on a State Farm

Over the last year or two, I had made up my mind to study agriculture at the university and then take over one of the large state farms and become a rich landowner. I would meet a rich young man who would also be an accomplished agriculturist, marry him and live happily ever after on my own estate just like the couples I knew from operettas, such as *Graefin Marizza* by Emmerich Calman, or from some movies I had seen. I was sure of a happy, rosy future.

My parents and I had inquired about the possibility of such a line of work and found out that there was a prerequisite of having to work in a practical capacity for the period of two years on a large farm before the university would accept any student into this faculty. During this last year my mother had written on my behalf to several state farms whose addresses she had procured. One of them had written back to acknowledge that they needed an apprentice and had asked me to come for an interview. My father, of course, was still in Lissa, so it was left to my mother to make all the arrangements. I was much too inexperienced and inhibited to undertake the necessary steps. All I knew was that I wanted to go to university and that I would do whatever it took to get me there.

So, soon after I was dismissed from the RAD my mother and I took the train to get to this interview in Thurow near the town of Anklam.

It actually was not far from Tenzerow where I had spent the previous summer in the work camp. From Anklam to Thurow, you had to take a narrow gauge train that looked as though it would topple over each time it went around a bend. It was almost like a doll's train.

My first impression of the estate was overwhelming. It was just as I had seen it in the movies: a huge white house with a circular driveway in front that had a pond in the middle. The entrance hall was large and had a winding staircase going to the second floor. We were ushered into a huge room which was generally referred to as "the ballroom". It had windows and glass doors from floor to ceiling and opened up onto a large terrace overlooking a beautiful park-like garden. A large table in the middle had been set for lunch with all kinds of wonderful dishes, and we were introduced to the family.

There was the owner of the farm, Ernst Krose, a lean, tall man of 39 years (as I found out later), his wife—whose parents had owned the farm originally—his parents and his sister—whose husband was in the army—and her five-year-old daughter. Also at the table were two young men, one of whom was an apprentice by the last name of "Benzin". (I never got to know his first name, he was just "Benzin".) The second one was a little older, in his early 20s and was also only called by his last name "Leu" (pronounced Loy). I was introduced as *Fräulein Hartmann*" and that was what everyone always called me from then on.

According to the prevailing etiquette, there was no familiarity between any of us. Everyone except the little girl was addressed with the formal *"Sie"*, equivalent to the English "thou" or the French "vous". All were very friendly to my mother and me. We were given a tour of the mansion and my room was to be the one above the main entrance door, facing the pond and the large farmyard. I was duly impressed with the size and the opulence of the house and decided then and there that that was where I wanted to be and to learn. The interview had turned out to be very informal and at the end of our visit Mr. Krose offered me the position of an apprentice, which I gladly accepted, and which was to begin two weeks from that particular day.

At the beginning of the war, Mr. Krose had agreed to have his farm declared a so-called "State Farm". This entitled him to take on apprentices but he was also responsible for the productivity of the farm, which was of utmost importance during the war when food was rationed and the population, as well as the army, depended on the local economy. In return, Mr. Krose was exempted from service in the army.

Two other younger German men also worked on the farm. Both were responsible for the cows, of which there were about 150, and for the milk production. One older man was the head shepherd of several hundred sheep, another looked after the pigs and still another worked in the horse barn. These were the positions of responsibility.

Aside from these men, about 100 Polish workers, called *Schnitter*,[1] were housed in the village in stone barracks. Since 1939, they no longer were seasonal workers, but had been assigned full-time to this farm and worked mainly in the fields planting potatoes, weeding the crops and doing the harvesting. During the winter they helped in the barns, kept the yard clear of snow and loaded the produce, which had been preserved in long rows under straw and dirt, onto the train lorries. Another work crew consisted of 50 or 60 Russian prisoners of war, who lived in separate barracks and were guarded by two old German soldiers. About half of these men worked in the barns with the animals, while the others joined the workers in the fields.

The whole village consisted only of about a dozen semi-detached houses for the regular German farmhands and their families, and one detached building which had formerly been used as a schoolhouse. The widow of the teacher still lived in it with her 12-year-old son.

Because of the political developments and the end of the war in the spring of 1945, I never completed my two years of apprenticeship, but the year that I lived on this farm was indeed a very memorable one. My experience of strict discipline in the previous year at the work camp helped me a great deal at this time, and my sense of duty and responsibility was drilled into me even more. I had also gained some self-confidence and managed to hold my own among all those men.

1   From the German word "schneiden": to cut; these seasonal workers often had to cut the grain with a scythe.

The day started at 6 a.m., with a briefing after breakfast about the work that would have to be done that day and who was to look after which part of it. The work was divided in such a way that the three of us learned the farm management from every angle. I learned to ride a horse and often had to travel from field to field to check on the work of the *Schnitter*. At other times, I helped the "old Mr. Krose" as he was generally known, in the office with the books that he kept meticulously. I often worked in the cow barns.

One of my regular jobs was to draw the markings of every newborn calf into a register book. All the cows and horses on the farm were registered. I learned to milk the cows, which was still done by hand. I drove a tractor as well as wagons piled up high with grain or hay drawn by four horses, learned to plough the field in straight furrows behind two horses as well as pulling the plough behind the tractor, and I cut the grain and grass with a scythe. The latter only had to be done at the outer corners of the fields because the machines could not turn the outside sharp corners.

Something I was especially proud of was that I learned how to fix these large field machines when they broke down, or when new parts had to be inserted, such as twine for the binders. I even knew what to do when the threshing machine stopped.

In the fall, all ground crops such as potatoes, carrots, sugar beets and turnips had to be preserved in large prepared stacks covered with straw and dirt as described earlier, and tons of it would be loaded on the train and shipped out for general distribution. When foals, calves or lambs were born, I often assisted. Sometimes it meant no sleep at all. I certainly learned a lot.

The three men, Ernst Krose, Leu and Benzin liked to play all kinds of tricks on me. On the day I learned to ride a horse, Mr. Krose led the horse out of the barn, held his hands together and asked me to step into them and pull myself up. As I did this he gave me such a boost that I fell off the horse on the other side, landing in the manure pit which was just outside the horse barn. Of course he had told all the workers in the barn to come and watch me ride. They all had great fun at my expense, but I tried again and stayed on the horse the second time.

One day the pigs had to be weighed. Leu wanted to know how much I weighed, so I stepped on the scale and turned out to weigh 200 pounds. I heard about this for a long time afterward. Another time I discovered in the morning when I made my bed that I had slept with a dead snake all night long. My room had a hanging lamp with a cord that I had to pull to turn on the light. When I did this one dark evening I grabbed a fluttering bat that they had attached to the cord. I did not think that that was very funny.

Still another time when I wanted to take a bath I found a piglet in the bathtub, which meant that I had to get dressed again, take it to the barn and then clean up the bathtub before I could use it. But it was all in good fun; they certainly paid me a lot of attention and I was able to laugh with them, which took the wind out of their sails.

The grains were stored in one of the many barn buildings. They had two floors, each one covered with enormous piles of all kinds of grains and feed for the animals. I learned to distinguish one from the other, to know when, how and where they had to be sown, which grain was selected for improvement and which animals were fed which feed, why, and how much. There also was always a contingent of people who had to go into the bush to cut some trees out that had been marked before, or to plant new trees. With this group I learned which trees were to be left standing and which trees needed to be cut down and why, and then I learned how to cut down the trees myself, handling the saws and ax like everybody else.

We also had a carpenter and a blacksmith on the premises. When the horses needed to be shod I often held their legs up while the blacksmith hammered the horseshoes on. I really loved the work on the farm, though sometimes it was absolutely exhausting. I knew, though, that I did not have to do the heavy work for the rest of my life, that this was just a learning period and that I needed to have tried everything myself before I could tell others what to do. Best of all, I liked the smell on the farm, the mixture of fresh air, cut grass or hay and animals. It smelled like Brietzig, which was home, and made me feel contented and secure.

CHAPTER FOUR

Escape from Brietzig

At Christmas in 1944, Mr. Krose gave me two weeks of holidays and I went home to Brietzig. This was the very last time I was ever to be there while it was still my home, which of course, I did not know at the time.

It also was the very last time that I would see my father, who had come with my brother from Lissa to spend Christmas with the family. It was a very somber time for all of us. I remember how disappointed and almost angry I was because I could not occupy my old room, since it, and my brother's room, had been turned over to two ladies who were refugees from Estonia. I slept in the little room above the pantry and my brother had a cot in the old upstairs kitchen. Neither of us liked what had happened, but we still didn't really see the seriousness of the situation. Although we knew at that time that many battles had been lost in the east and west, the front was a long way away from us and it did not even occur to me that soon we would lose not just our home, but the village and the land and everything I had known until this time.

My brother, Juergen, who was 16 years old at this time, had been drafted the previous year to dig trenches on the eastern front.[1] He was

---

[1]   Juergen has written his biography as well, and told about the tough times of his teenage years.

stationed not very far away from Lissa and once in awhile my father was able to visit with him. They both had managed to return home this year for Christmas. Thinking back to it, I am sure that my parents knew how desperate the situation was for Germany. I remember feeling very sad and uneasy, especially on the day when my father and brother returned to Lissa. The three of us left Brietzig on the same train and stayed together until we went in different directions in Stettin. I took a train west to Anklam; they took the one that went east to Posen, back in the direction of the front, while my mother stayed back home in Brietzig.

In the following two weeks, the Russian army approached so quickly toward Lissa and Posen that my father went to fetch my brother and abandoned everything in Lissa to return to Brietzig. This in itself was not an easy task. It took them almost a week to get home. They partly rode on a train, then walked, thumbed their way on wagon rides, walked some more, got a ride on a locomotive without a train behind it and spent the nights in railroad stations, barns or wherever there was a roof over their heads.

Upon their arrival in Brietzig there awaited a letter addressed to my brother from the military, ordering him to report immediately to a training camp in Bavaria. I can just imagine the agony my parents must have gone through trying to decide whether to let him go or to keep him with them. But they probably knew that the Russians would soon be in Brietzig and figured he may be safer in Bavaria, which seemed a long way off to the southwest, so they let him go after a day or two.

It was now the latter part of January, 1945. As the war front came closer and closer, the people in Brietzig began to load their belongings onto wagons, preparing to evacuate the village. One of our neighbour farmers had offered my parents a wagon and two horses. They packed all our belongings in boxes and crates and loaded them on this wagon, ready to leave with everybody else. But it was not to be. The Russian army advanced so fast that no one had a chance to get out. The desperation and fear of the village people must have been horrific.

On the 30th of January 1945, which was my 20th birthday, I received a telephone call in Thurow from my mother. She told me in a breaking voice that she was at the train station in Anklam and wondered if I could possibly come to pick her up. I remember this day as if it were just a week ago. It was cold and overcast and a lot of snow was on the ground. I asked Mr. Krose for permission to take the sleigh and get my mother, to which he immediately agreed. I hitched the horse to the sleigh and took off, almost numb with fear and foreboding. There was not a soul on the road, just the horse and I, and I had a sinking feeling in my stomach. As I neared Anklam I saw this lonely figure approaching, dark against the snow, carrying a bag in each hand. It was my mother. She had started walking toward Thurow after the phone call she had made to me and here we met in the middle of a deserted road on a bitterly cold day in January, amidst snow-covered fields as far as the eye could see. Many years later I saw the movie *Dr. Zhivago* and it reminded me of our own fate and our sad experiences. I bundled my mother up in blankets that I had brought with me and turned the sleigh around. My first question was: "Where is *Vati*?" She could hardly speak when she said that he had stayed in Brietzig because he felt that he could not cowardly desert the other villagers.

Slowly I heard the whole story: The day before, they all had heard the guns and cannon fire from the front, which had approached the neighbouring village of Kossin. The train had stopped coming through the village for the last week and they had heard that only infrequently were some trains leaving the town of Pyritz in the northwesterly direction to Stettin. Rumours were running rampant through the village, saying the Russians had cut off all roads that would lead toward the west and that escape was impossible. The village elders decided that they all were going to stay.

•

THE BUERGERMEISTER, THAT IS, THE MAYOR, Fritz Schulz, was the only person left in the village with a telephone. The German army, or what was left of it, had taken over local command and the various mayors of the villages were obliged to stay in contact with the army commander, and had to report what went on in their villages.

In return they were informed of the location of the advancing Russian army. Fritz Schulz knew that as soon as the Russians entered our village, he would be the first one for whom they would come looking. He needed some help. So he asked my father if he would stand by him and in turn he proposed that both of their wives should leave the village if that was still possible. He had heard that there was one more train leaving Pyritz on the 30th of January, which was more than likely going to be the very last one and therefore the last chance for anyone to escape. He had decided that he was going to take his wife and daughter, Gretchen, who at the time was about 22 years old, with his horse drawn sleigh to Pyritz. My father immediately agreed to send his wife, my mother, with them, and the two men and three women left Brietzig before dawn on January 30 1945, to cover the 10-kilometre distance to the train station in Pyritz.

All the pleading of the women to their husbands to come with them was for naught; the men felt that they could not desert the rest of the villagers who no longer had any opportunity to escape, even though all of them had packed their belongings on wagons that were ready to leave. It was too late! So with tears streaming down their faces they said their goodbyes, the men pushed their wives into the ice cold, overcrowded train and then returned to Brietzig, never to be reunited with their families again.

•

THE TRAIN BROUGHT THE REFUGEES to Stettin where my mother parted company from the two other women and managed to find a train that left for Anklam from where she had called me. I have often wondered why not everyone had taken one of the last trains. Most of them could probably have saved themselves, but I suppose the idea of leaving their home, which had been theirs for generations, and all their belongings, was just an unthinkable prospect. Besides, nobody seriously thought that the Russians would ever be able to come this far west anyway—

until the 29th of January, when the villagers heard the cannon shots all around them and saw the Russian planes overhead. Be that as it may, everyone in the village stayed except for the three women.

On the 31st of January, the Russian army approached the village from Kossin, about three or four kilometres east of Brietzig. They came across the fields and along the dirt road at the south end at the foot of the *Wartberg*, the same road that Bishop Otto von Bamberg had taken in the 12th Century when he baptized the first Christians in the area.

It was not until 1989, 44 years after the war ended, that I found out that my father had saved our village from total destruction. Frieda, our former babysitter and friend, visited me in Canada and relayed the events of that day: Of the German army, no soldier had remained in the area. All the neighbours had huddled together in the house across the street from ours; Frieda and my father were among them. No one knew what to do and how to escape these horrors of war. My father decided to attach a white bed sheet to a long pole and walk across the field toward the approaching enemy army, indicating that the villagers were not going to fight back. Since no one wanted to join him, he got up the courage to go alone on this mission. Frieda told me that the people in the house did not expect to see him alive again. One of them said: "Hartmann is crazy." The church and a few houses had already been damaged the day before by cannon fire. Because of the surrender that my father indicated, no further damage was done to structures in the village.

Though no fires were set at that time, the people suffered horrendously. The looting and plundering were minor evils compared to the raping and torturing that went on for weeks and months as ever new troops arrived from the east. Almost all of my former girlfriends contracted syphilis; many died very young. Eventually, during April and May, all but the very sick or old and children under the age of 10, were loaded onto trucks and transported to Siberia, southeast of Lake Baikal, including my father. Many of the men and women did not arrive there alive. Fritz Schulz and our Lutheran minister died on the way and were unceremoniously thrown out of the freight cars by the Russian patrols. Some of the buildings in the village were burned down at that time, but most of them remained standing and are there to this day, except for the old thatched farmhouses I described earlier. Our house, too, remained standing and is still there, though it has been whitewashed.

War Reaches Thurow

IN THE MEANTIME MY MOTHER remained with me in Thurow where we both shared my room. She tried to make herself useful around the house, but there was really not much for her to do since there were enough maids to take care of everything. She finally ended up giving piano lessons to the six-year-old niece of Mr. Krose, who had not the slightest interest in learning to play. We listened every day to the radio reports and heard that the Russians had come farther and farther to the west, that Pyritz had been burned to the ground and that they were approaching Stettin. This was about the middle of February. The big river Oder at Stettin was a natural barrier and for several weeks the Russian army was delayed there. By March it began to thaw and the Russians crossed the Oder into Vorpommern, the western part of the province. We were about 40 or 50 kilometres west of Stettin.

At that time we had no idea what had happened to my father or any of the people back home, nor did we get any message from my brother Juergen. The last my mother knew of him was that he had been sent into a training camp in Bavaria. The mail had stopped coming through and we were dependent entirely on the radio reports. We began to notice more and more planes flying overhead; sometimes they were Russian bombers that flew very low and began to shoot with what must have been machine guns. We had begun to plow the fields and prepare them for sowing and I remember the horrible feeling lying flat on the ground in a furrow or a ditch while the planes flew over us, either shooting at each other or at us.

Mr. Krose called all the village people together and ordered them to pack their valuables, clothing and bedding on wagons which he provided. There were maybe 60 people, almost all of them women and children, whose home was Thurow, and about 100 refugees who had drifted in during the last several months, and who all had their own horses and wagons. Every available room in each house was occupied by these refugees while hundreds of prisoners of war—French, English, Russians, Poles—filled the haylofts and barns.

By this time the refugees usually stayed just a few days on the farm and then marched westward in seemingly never-ending columns. During the last several months of 1944, the Poles and the Russian prisoners of war had been ordered to build a dozen or so makeshift houses out of loam, in which the overflow of refugees were now housed.

All through April we continued with our regular daily chores, even planted potatoes, but at the same time we were ready to leave at a moment's notice.

During the last nine months, Mrs. Krose had been pregnant with her second child—the first one had died at birth prior to my time on the farm. The birth was expected at the end of March. One night we heard a terrible commotion downstairs, carriages were coming and going and there was a lot of running about. When we came down the next morning we were told that the baby, a boy, had been born, but both mother and baby had died. This was just another terrible thing that happened on top of all the anxiety and stress that we all felt. For two days mother and child lay in the large hall for friends and family to come and say goodbye. On the third day they were buried in the family plot on the estate. Mrs. Krose had been born in this house and died in it, and in the end, she was the only one of all the people there who remained in Thurow.

Things went from bad to worse. In April, we could hear the rumblings of war coming closer. Reports on the radio informed us that the Russian army had crossed the Oder and was approaching Anklam. Late one evening Mr. Krose, Leu, Benzin and I buried a very large wooden box with valuables in one of the barns several feet under the dirt floor. Each day the tension and fear grew. Each day more refugees arrived for a short time and moved on the following day; each day our wagons were checked and secured and by the end of April, all POWs had disappeared except for our own. A foreboding atmosphere hung over the whole village.

Then on April 28th, in the middle of the night at 2 a.m. Mr. Krose knocked on our door and called: "It's time to go. Get ready. Meet me downstairs."

At this point began for me a time period through which I lived almost as if in a sleepwalk. It is strange how one can live almost as an onlooker to one's own life, which is filled with bizarre incidents, fear, hope, horror, adventure and tenacious determination to survive.

•

AS SOON AS I WAS DRESSED I ran downstairs, leaving my mother behind to gather the last few belongings we had to put on our designated wagon. Mr. Krose had gathered Leu, Benzin and the foremen, a total of about 10 people including myself as the only woman. We listened to his orders: one was assigned to arouse the people, the rest of us went to the cow barn where we untied all the cows and opened all the doors wide for them to leave and fend for themselves. Then some of us opened the sheep barn doors, while the others unlocked all pig pen doors. Following that we got the horses and hitched them to the wagons which were all packed, standing in the middle of the large barnyard around the pond. Four oxen pulled two wagons with fodder for the horses and we hitched a few cows to the end of some wagons to have milk for the children.

By 6 o'clock in the morning all was ready. We took a last glance at the manor house and left in a caravan of about 20 wagons. The Polish workers had put their few belongings on one wagon, as did the Russian POWs, who all marched in a column behind us under the guard of the two old gun-carrying soldiers.

My mother and I had been assigned to share a wagon with one of the refugee women from East Prussia, who had stayed in Thurow with her six-year-old son since autumn. She had arrived with her own horse and wagon together with a young Russian POW who had escaped with her. His name was Ivan and he had learned to speak German fluently. He was about my age and was a very handsome, friendly young man. Despite the fact that it was strictly forbidden to talk to POWs except in regard to their work, I had talked with Ivan frequently and was fascinated by what he told me about Russia and his own life.

He came from Kiev, had gone to school there and was dragged into the army against his will as soon as the war started, when he was 17 years old. He had never been allowed to write to his parents and had no idea what had become of them. Very early during the war he had become a prisoner of war and was sent to East Prussia to help this German farmer's wife, whose husband was in the German army. Ivan was terrified of being captured by the Russian army, since all Russian soldiers had been ordered to fight to their death and never allow themselves to be taken prisoner. In Thurow, Ivan had been free to come and go; the German woman considered him part of her family. Over a period of a few weeks, he and I had become friends. It went as far as the two of us having taken several bike rides together along the country lanes and sharing a picnic by the road side. When I was young, a kiss meant commitment and was a big emotional experience, so it never happened between us. However, we both liked each other.

Now, on this day in late April 1945, Ivan was the driver on our wagon and was responsible for the horses. My mother, the woman and her young son were riding on it, while I rode my bicycle beside the trek, delivering orders from Mr. Krose in the front to Leu and Benzin who were positioned at the end and in the middle respectively. We headed in the western direction with the intention of reaching Rostock and eventually crossing the river Elbe into the western part of the country, where we knew that the Americans were advancing. We felt that it would be better to meet our fate and the end of the war facing the Americans and the English rather than falling into the hands of the Russian troops.

At first we made good headway until we came to the main highway. There we met up with hundreds of other treks and thousands of people who were fleeing towards the west. There were wagons upon wagons, civilians with hand-drawn carts, columns of POWs and columns of German soldiers, sometimes going in both directions, to and away from the front lines.

Military vehicles of all sorts and sizes, and soldiers on horseback demanded space on the road. I remember a feeling of excitement and bravery as I juggled myself on my bicycle through this mass of desperate and disorganized humanity, trying to help keep our group together and piloting lost villagers back to our trek. Whenever military cars, trucks, tanks or motorcycles passed by, everybody had to move over to the side, often into the ditch because the road was not really a highway, just a paved two-lane street. On the first day we managed about 30 kilometres, from then on it became slower and slower and the mass of fleeing people became larger at every crossroad.

There were people behind and in front of us as far as the eye could see, a slowly crawling trail of misery. The whole atmosphere was one of horror, fear and anxiety. Rumours began to circulate about a new miracle weapon that would be used within a day or two and the enemy armies would be destroyed. Then again horror stories were whispered from one wagon to another about the atrocities that had been committed by the Russian troops in the cities and villages they had conquered.

On the fourth day we passed through the city of Demmin. I remember the chaos in the streets, everybody seemed to be getting ready to join the fleeing masses. Stores were open and people just walked in and picked up groceries of whatever was left. It was not a scene of looting, nobody was fighting or trying to grab more than what was needed for the moment. Since we were well-prepared and had enough food supplies on our wagons to last us for several weeks, we did not stop.

On the following day we halted outside the city for the night. Our way had taken us past my former work camp, Tenzerow. I took a quick detour on my bike to see what had happened there. All the doors were unlocked when I arrived but not a soul was left in the house. I hurried back to our trek. Shortly thereafter the road rose up and we came onto a fairly high hill. As we turned to look back we saw the city of Demmin in flames.

We now knew that we were running out of time. People began to become more panicky and wanted to rush past the slow-moving wagons ahead of us, but there was just no way. The road was covered from side to side with people and vehicles and the fields to the right and left were muddy from the last spring rains. Any wagon would have gotten hope-lessly stuck in it.

At the end of this day we stopped beside a big barn on the outskirts of a village where other treks had already sought some shelter for the night. As Mr. Krose walked along the row of our wagon group he was spotted by a man who called him by name. As it turned out, it was the owner of one of the neighbouring state farms, who together with his family and the villagers of his estate, had also left and taken the same direction as we: west. The two men and their families had been friends and decided to travel together from here on. Mr. Krose's family now consisted of his parents and his sister with her daughter, while the other man had a wife, three children—two girls and one boy—all under 10 years of age, and his mother-in-law. His trek also consisted of about 20 wagons.

On the next day we all tried to stay as one group: we now were a trek of about 40 wagons that sort of belonged together. I again was the courier on my bicycle, riding from front to back and vice versa, trying to keep everyone together while dodging horses, tanks, motorcycles and walking people. This day we heard for the first time that Hitler appar-ently was dead. One of the soldiers shouted it from a truck as it moved past us. I still waited for some miracle to happen that would allow us to go back to our homes.

More and more German troops began to drive past in both directions, causing our wagon trains to stop, and forcing the people who walked into the ditches. We heard shooting behind and in front of us and now air-planes began to fly over us, which we could identify as Russian planes.

This was the fifth day since we had left Thurow and we were still heading in the direction of Rostock. I did not have access to a map and did not realize that we were still many kilometres southeast of that city. By the afternoon we passed through Dargun and still everyone hoped and prayed that we would get close to the American front line. But as the day went on, people began to come running toward us, back to the east, from where we had just come. Horrified and frightened, they were say-ing that they had been at the front line and that there was no way to get through to the west. Apparently there was gunfire everywhere and worst of all, the Russian planes were flying very low, shooting at everything that moved on or beside any road.

As more and more people came running toward us, all screaming the same frightening story, there was no reason for us to doubt them. Mr. Krose and his friend, the two trek leaders, decided that we would turn off the main road to the left onto a narrow dirt road that led into a dense forest. This dirt road went slightly uphill for about two kilometres. By the time our 40 or so wagons had reached the top it began to get dark and we halted. We could hear shooting going on close by and it was decided that we would stay at least for the night in this forest. The wagons were arranged in two rows, half on the right and half on the left of the sandy road so that a narrow walkway remained in the middle. All wagons had round canvas covers and looked very much like the North American Conestoga wagons. So far, the weather had been cool but dry. As the evening progressed, the shooting stopped and we all slept in our wagons.

The next morning, two of the men were sent to climb some high trees as lookouts. They reported that they could see the main road and that the Russian army was marching along it. They had also seen trucks, tanks and horses, all moving in the western direction. We now knew that they had caught up with us and the rest of the fleeing population, and that we were trapped. There was nothing we could do but wait in quiet anxiety and pray.

•

AT ABOUT 10 O'CLOCK THE FOLLOWING morning we heard a motorcycle approaching from ahead of us. Out of the forest there appeared a young Russian soldier. As he suddenly found himself in the middle of a large group of German people, he must have been as stunned and frightened as we were. He stopped, looked around, then smiled at some of us and left. We knew now that we had been discovered and that most likely others would follow. Sure enough, at about one o'clock in the afternoon a whole cavalry came riding up the sandy path from the main road. They circled around our wagon camp and then closed in on us. We had all taken cover in our wagons but were immediately ordered with shouts and gestures to come out and line up in the middle of the path. Some of the soldiers had gotten off their horses and pushed all the men and boys over to one side, while the mounted soldiers pointed their guns at us.

While this was happening, my mother suddenly grabbed my hand and started to run with me past the horses into the forest. We did not get very far because one of the riders fired a bullet in our direction and then rode in front of us, pushing us back into the lineup with the men. One of the soldiers spoke some German and ordered all the women and children back onto the wagons, then he dismissed the Poles and the Russian prisoners of war to their camp site. Eventually he yelled something at my mother and me, and motioned for us to disappear to our wagon, which we only too gladly did.

Mr. Krose, his father, his friend and the few other German men, as well as all the boys from about 11 or 12 years up, were marched off without being given the chance to say goodbye to their families. The horsemen left with them, leaving us behind, terror-stricken and in utter despair. The Poles began to leave the camp on foot, just disappearing into the forest. The Russian prisoners of war were still there, too afraid and confused to know what to do. Ivan informed us that they had been told to stay where they were.

In the afternoon it began to rain and finally it poured. Each of us huddled in our wagon, cold, damp and afraid. The walkway in the middle of the camp had turned to mud; it was a dismal situation. Around 6 p.m. we heard Russian shouting and singing coming in our direction. About 10 horse drawn coaches appeared with two or three Russian soldiers in each, most of them appearing to be drunk. They went from one of our wagons to the next and dragged all young girls and women out and forced them into the coaches. They kept on repeating the German words for "party" and "dancing" over and over. I had hidden in the back of our wagon under blankets together with my mother and the other young woman. Ivan sat at the front. One of the soldiers came close and forced us to come forward. He did not want my mother, but was about to take the woman and me, when Ivan spoke to him in an angry voice. The soldier looked at me, motioned me back and took the mother of the six-year-old boy with him. When I later asked Ivan what he had said to the soldier, he told me that he had told him that he and I were engaged to be married, and that he had no right to take me. I guess my guardian angel was again looking out for me that day.

After they had left, Ivan wrote a note in Russian and gave it to me with the instruction to show it to any Russian soldier who was going to take me with him. He explained that he had written on it that I was engaged to a high-ranking Russian officer and that nobody was to touch me. He then signed it with some officer's name. I kept that note for years until it fell apart, but during those terrible months, twice I had reason to use it, and twice I was let go.

The night that followed was absolutely horrible. From every wagon came crying voices, sometimes screams. The wife of Mr. Krose's friend, who also had been spared for some reason, was so distraught that she tried to kill herself and her three children. She had taken a knife and cut the wrists of the children and of herself. The screams of the children alerted the rest of us. We found them all lying in a puddle of blood but still alive. There was an old midwife on one of the wagons who managed to stop the bleeding of the mother and the two older girls, but for the little boy it was too late. He died that night and we buried him in the morning.

Very early the following morning a large contingency of soldiers in wagons and on horseback returned the girls and women they had taken with them the evening before. All of them had been raped. The soldiers ordered the Russian prisoners of war into the middle of the camp, lined them up and then marched them into the forest. Shortly thereafter, we heard shots, many shots. They had killed their own people, including my Ivan.

It did not take long and the soldiers were back at our camp. This time they took all the strongest and best horses from our wagons and left us with only the old or very young ones. They plundered a few of the wagons and then gave us to understand that we had to be gone by the next morning at 10 o'clock or else we would be shot as well.

CHAPTER FIVE

First Return to Thurow

Since we did not have a leader anymore to make decisions for the group or to be in command, I felt I had to do something about it. So I called all the women together and the remainder of the Polish people who were still with us and suggested to them all, that anybody who wished to leave on their own should do so now, while I had decided to return to Thurow and would be willing to lead the first wagon for those who wanted to return with me. I told them that we would have to double up and that we could only take a total of five wagons back because only a few horses were left. Most of the Poles decided to leave and did so on foot with whatever they could carry. The German people almost all wanted to return to their village, including the wife of Mr. Krose's friend, with her remaining two children.

During the few hours of daylight that were left, we repacked our wagons and threw out everything that was not absolutely needed. There must have been a treasure lying at the side of the path in that forest. I remember that, with much regret, I threw away my one and only, almost new pair of Sunday shoes. They were of maroon-coloured leather with blue suede decorations.

I chose which horses were to pull the wagons and which ones were to be used as spares, and after staying one more night in the forest we left at dawn in a southeasterly direction, avoiding the main road and travelling only on dirt roads that connected the villages.

I had piled my hair up high and hid it under a cap, my face was dirty from dust that I had rubbed in to appear as ugly as possible, and I wore my regular working attire: "bridges"—a kind of riding pant, a jacket and knee-high leather boots. Thus equipped, I drove the first wagon, leading our small trek back to where we had come from. Four of the women whose husbands had been taken away drove the other wagons, each of them carrying more people than belongings.

We had not gone more than an hour or two when a small band of Russians stopped us, entered our wagons, waving their guns at us and took whatever they wanted. At this encounter I lost my little accordion which I cherished and loved to play. I guess it was not absolutely necessary.

One thing that survived this and all previous and following pillages was the golden pocket watch of my father. My mother had brought it with her in January when she left Brietzig—together with some jars of preserved cherries. I remember reproaching her at that time for not having saved our old family bible or some of the many photographs so that we might have a memory of our home. Under tears she had explained to me that everything had been packed in boxes, ready to be loaded onto wagons with which to flee from the Russian front. It was not meant to be.

However, this watch was safe. My mother had wrapped it in several layers of leather and immersed it into a pail of sugar beet syrup. In this container (later in a smaller jar), it made it all the way to West Germany and is now in the possession of my brother Juergen in Denver, who can one day pass it on to his oldest son.

Later, on this first day of our trek back, we were stopped once more. The wagons were searched and plundered again and I realized that we had to change our strategy. It was a horrible feeling having to be afraid every minute of sudden hold-ups, never knowing what they might do to us. I decided then and there, that from now on we had to hide during the day and only travel during the night. We found hiding places behind burnt out houses and barns, behind large haystacks that stood in the fields, or in between bushes.

One day we came by a deserted *Gutshaus*, which is the German word for a large estate house, almost like a mansion. We stayed on that property during the day and ventured into the house. It was empty, but one window was still covered by hanging curtains. Like Scarlett O'Hara, of whom I had never heard at that time, I tore them down and later on, my mother made a dress out of them for me.

During those days, on the way back, we passed repulsive sights of dead animals, dead soldiers and dead civilians. The weather began to get warm and the stench in the air was sickening. Nobody had as yet buried the dead and we could not do it either because we did not have any tools with us. We saw very few living people on our way back to Thurow. Those still alive hid during the day and mostly during the night as well. Once or twice in the evening I knocked on some door that looked like a farmer's house and asked for some milk or something to eat. People were extremely helpful and shared of whatever little they had left, just as we all shared our common misery.

•

BY THE END OF MAY WE ARRIVED back in Thurow, after having been caught again and detained for several days in a makeshift camp with hundreds of other refugees. It was here that I had to make use of the paper that Ivan had given me and thanked his spirit for having saved me again. Eventually the Russians had to let us go since there was neither food nor water for all the detainees. The people from the neighbouring village returned to their own homes and we faced the destruction that had taken place in Thurow.

We had approached the village with great caution, not knowing whether Russian troops might be there, but we were lucky—no human was in sight. At first we ventured into the main house of the Krose mansion. From the kitchen area we heard screams, and found in the adjacent locked walk-in freezer a half-starved, half-frozen, half-crazed German soldier and the stabbed German shepherd dog that had been left behind. In the middle of the kitchen lay a dead pig, the whole house was vandalized beyond description. All the beds were slashed, feathers fly-ing around everywhere, the curtains, chairs and the remaining furniture was smashed and pieces lay everywhere.

The old Mrs. Krose, Ernst's mother, who had always been used to command and to being served, demanded of us to help her clean up the house, but none of us felt so inclined as we thought that that would be a very dumb thing to do. I was certain that sooner or later marauding troops would arrive again and the first place they would look would be the main house. Mrs. Krose wished to move back into the house to-gether with her husband, whom the Russians had not taken. He was at that time at least 75 years old and almost completely deaf. Mrs. Krose actually did stay in the house that first night but in the evening of the second day a group of soldiers chased her out. That experience changed her mind and she joined the rest of us. We had decided not to stay in any of the houses, but in the evenings we climbed up into the hayloft, pulled up the ladder and for the following three months spent the nights there. Each time wandering soldier hordes arrived in the evening or during the night we hardly dared to breathe and were as quiet as mice.

During the days we always posted a look-out, either in a tree or mostly in the attic of the main house because that was the highest loca-tion from which one could easily overlook the four roads that led into the village. Whenever there was some movement spotted the look-out would give a loud sign by hooting like an owl and we would all run into the barn and scramble up into the hayloft. The plundering hordes usu-ally did not stay very long since there was nothing of value left that they could take. Our last personal belongings we had immediately stored in the hayloft as well, so the main house and all the workers' houses were empty, except for some wooden beds, with no sheets and blankets, and some tables and chairs.

When things were quiet during the day we tried to fetch some food for ourselves as best we could. We went into the nearby fields and dug up some of the crops that had either been sown before we left or that still lay preserved in large straw and dirt mounds from the previous year, such as potatoes, carrots, sugar beets and turnips. In the barns there remained large mounds of grains of different kinds, which we ground into flour and porridge. Barley grains, smashed and roasted, would make a tasty cup of "coffee". Sugar beet shavings served as sweetener and the raw salt that was stored for the horses and cows to lick on, we crushed, washed out the dirt and used to spice our meager meals.

There was no sign of any of the animals. We could not find any of the cows, sheep or pigs; we only had the horses which had pulled our wagons back. They, of course, had to be fed and watered, which I did three times a day with the occasional help of some young boys. At that time I had to work harder than any time before or after in all my life. The water had to be brought into the barn to the horses from the pump in the yard. I had to carry two wooden buckets filled with water attached to a yoke which I had placed over my shoulders. Every day there had to be three waterings of the twelve horses which meant I had to take the trip to and from the pump at least twenty times a day, sometimes more than that. Every day I filled sacks full of grain that was stored on the upper floor in the barn about 200 metres away from the stable. I carried these sacks across my shoulder down the stairs and across the yard to the stable where the horses were tied.

One day in late August the men who had been taken away from us in the forest in May, suddenly reappeared, including Mr. Krose, Leu and Benzin. They had been held captive somewhere with other civilians but finally were released without explanation. Their assumption was that the Russians just did not know what to do with all the prisoners. When we asked them about details of the past several weeks, they refused to talk about it.

We still spent the nights in the hayloft and still posted look-outs during the day. However, since nothing terrible had happened for a while, our look-out must have become a bit careless because one day we suddenly heard him shout that several Russians were at the entrance to the village. This of course meant that they were practically upon us and only two or three minutes away.

It was early in the morning and I remember hearing his shout while I was standing in my underwear in a small room beside the stable washing myself. I held a washcloth in my hand and for some reason I grabbed my toothbrush and the toothpaste and jumped out of the small window that faced the garden of the main house. There was no time for any of us to run to the hayloft and climb up the ladder. All the women ran into some hiding place wherever they could find one. I was desperate to find a place where I could hide. I was not good at climbing trees and the bushes were not thick enough to hide me. As I looked around in fear I spotted an old rain barrel under the spout that ran down from the roof. It was about three feet high and two feet in diameter and had a broken wooden lid on it. Without further thinking I climbed in and pulled the broken piece of wood over my head. It was not a minute too soon for I heard footsteps coming toward me and the conversation of two Russians. Suddenly I realized that I had dropped my washcloth and toothbrush in my anxiety when I climbed into the barrel. My heart pounded so loud, I thought they could hear it as I heard them stop only a few feet away from my barrel. I could sense that one had picked up my utensils and they were wondering how these things had gotten there.

The Russians stood there for the longest time, then they walked a few steps away, came back, talked some more and repeated this several times. Meanwhile I had noticed that my feet were all wet. As I opened my eyes I realized there was about half a foot of dirty water in the barrel and that bugs and spiders were crawling along the sides. I could not move and had no protection against all the insects. Still, this was a minor evil against the thought that these men would find me crouched down, wearing nothing but my underwear. Actually I wasn't quite sure what they in fact could or would do to me, I just knew that it must be horrible, maybe they would torture and kill me. During those months the fear penetrated the air like a black blanket; it was like a contagious epidemic illness that had affected me and every living soul.

Eventually I heard them leave the area, but I was too shell-shocked to move. The insects in the barrel meanwhile had become used to their new inmate and were crawling all over me. I was afraid to slap them for fear it would make a noise and besides the barrel was so small that I virtually was not able to move. After about half an hour or forty minutes

I heard my mother calling me and knew that now the danger was over. My limbs were so stiff that I could not stand up. Somehow, my mother pulled me out, but I fell over, dragging the barrel, the dirty water and the bugs with me.

This was the first time in my life that I completely lost my nerves. I shrieked and screamed and carried on and felt that I could not live another day of this terrible life. It took me a long time to calm down. My mother who was just as distraught as I was, tried her best to comfort me. She made me wash off the dirt and talked to me as though I were an infant and as though she could make all the hurt go away—only we both knew that it would not.

This particular story does not end here either. After I had gotten hold of myself again she told me that some of the soldiers had found my clothes which I had left behind as I jumped out of the window. They had asked Benzin, who just happened to be nearby, where the girl was to whom the clothes belonged. He had pointed them in the opposite direction toward a little wooded area. They had searched there everywhere and of course did not find me. They returned in a rage and beat up Benzin mercilessly. It took several days for us to nurse him back to health. I certainly owed him a great debt and was very grateful that he had not pointed them in my direction.

From that day on our look-outs were again much more vigilant and with good reason. Practically every second day marauding groups of soldiers came through the village searching through houses and stealing whatever was not nailed down. Each time all the women would scramble again into some hiding spots, the safest of them still was the hayloft into which we retreated when there was enough time. During all those weeks, nobody ventured too far away from the rest of the villagers. If we needed food from the fields we went during the night and in groups.

On another one of these occasions I happened to be in the loft of the grain barn preparing food for the horses when I heard the warning sound of the hooting owl. I did not want to take any chances by running out, so I dug myself into one of the grain heaps. It did not take long and I heard several Russians come up the stairs. The sound of their voices always made my skin crawl. I lay still without moving a muscle and then heard how they poked into the different grain heaps with their bayonets. I must have had a very attentive guardian angel who protected me again from being discovered. After a time that seemed like eternity to me, they left, leaving me in fear, frustration and despair. I could hear my mother's voice just below the barn talking to what sounded like a female Russian voice. This drove me out of my hiding place and as I looked through one of the openings between some planks I saw my mother with a female Russian soldier who seemed to have taken something away from my mother, which she tried to beg back from her. After several minutes the woman gave a bag to my mother, which, I found out later, contained some odds and ends of our last few belongings, among them photographs from home which I had kept in Thurow during my time as apprentice. The woman had returned the photos to my mother but kept the other things, whatever they were. Some of those photographs appear in this book.

None of us ever knew from where these plundering hordes would come. Sometimes they arrived on bikes, sometimes in military vehicles, sometimes on horseback and sometimes even on foot. It seems that they were given free range to comb the countryside and grab, rob, steal and plunder whatever they wanted.

After several more weeks, things calmed down and we all decided to move into the empty houses of the former farm workers. This meant that some women and children would move back into their original dwellings. Mr. Krose, his parents, his sister and daughter moved into one of the temporary mud houses and my mother and I settled in an upstairs room in the old schoolhouse. The former teacher's widow lived downstairs with her 12-year-old son. Each of us owned only the bare necessities: a blanket, maybe a few sheets and a pot or two, and we emptied the hayloft of what we had saved. It was amazing how helpful people had been with each other all through these awful months, except for the old Mrs. Krose, who was very angry, particularly at me, because I had not wanted to help her clean up the main house and be at her beck and call. She must have influenced her son after he returned with the other men because neither of them spoke to me again. I did not feel at all guilty about my actions and decisions because my first loyalty lay with my mother and besides that, I knew it was a ridiculous plan to live again in the main house.

We had reached the decision to move into the village houses just in time, for a day or two later a group of about 40 Russian soldiers moved into the big house. Had we remained in the hayloft we would have easily been seen from the house. It was obvious that they had been ordered to live there. We were not at all sure how this new development would affect us, but one of these men seemed to be in charge and that was more than what we had experienced before. At first we were all very fearful and did not leave the houses unless we had to. I still fed the horses in the stable on the property every morning around 5 a.m. and the house was still quiet at that time. In the evenings we always heard a lot of noise, singing and music. It seemed that a lot of partying and drinking went on in the building.

We all stayed as far away from the house as we could. However, the teacher's widow decided one late evening to sneak into the garden to get some vegetables that she knew had been planted in the early spring. Unfortunately for her she was caught by one of the soldiers. She returned 48 hours later and was a nervous wreck. She said that she had been locked up in the cellar, but who knows what happened to her in reality; she never spoke of the incident again.

CHAPTER SIX

Leaving Thurow a Second Time

Both my mother and I were very worried about my father in Brietzig, and about my brother. The postal service had broken down months ago, nobody owned a radio anymore and news was just not available. We had never officially been told that the war was over, we just knew that it was, and that Germany had lost. Some rumors of Hitler's death circulated but no one knew for sure what had happened or was happening anywhere else in the country. My mother and I discussed our situation and decided that since we had to live under the Russians in Thurow we might as well live under the Russians in Brietzig, where we belonged, and we might as well go back there. After thinking about this for a few days, we decided that this was what we were going to do..

One morning, I took the two best horses of those that were left, hitched them to a wagon, loaded our few things on it and off we went without telling anybody about it. We believed that now, at the beginning of September, things had gone back to some sort of order again.

The first stretch of the way went alright, but by about noon we encountered the first Russian band that took most of the food we had taken for our journey. They were not interested in the pail of sugar beet syrup in which the golden watch was still immersed. After this first encounter we realized again that we needed to travel during the night and hide during the day.

Toward the evening of the fourth day we set out again and came to a very steep downhill road. The horses were old to start with and every day they seemed to get slower. I had very great difficulty driving them down this steep hill. The wagon rolled faster than the horses could walk, even with the brakes on. Finally I got off the wagon and led them by the halter.

Halfway down the hill a carriage with Russian soldiers overtook us and stopped right in front of us, forcing me to stop as well. They got off their carriage, said something to us in Russian and looked at the horses. Despite my desperate protests they unhitched the better one of the two horses, tied it to the back of their carriage and left.

I was extremely upset and furious but neither tears nor hatred helped; we were left with one old horse that could hardly carry itself. After we had stopped crying about this lousy life, we knew that we would never be able to reach Brietzig. However, we had to get at least to the next village which happened to be Ferdinandshof. It was visible in the distance and wasn't all that far away. So I took the left side of the wagon shaft from which the horse had been taken in order to balance the wagon and keep it on the road. Our poor old horse tried the best it could but as we came close to Ferdinandshof it stopped and would not move again. We waited for a while but suddenly it dropped to the ground, fell over and died right there and then. I guess, it too, felt the desperation and hopelessness and did not see any more sense in going on. Both my mother and I could not cry any longer, there were just no more tears left.

There was nothing left for us to do but grab a few things in bags and walk to the village. When we arrived there, we found the village overflowing with refugees who had the same desire as we did, namely to go back East, to their home town or village from which they had fled weeks or months earlier. I remember that it was a very warm day, and since it was early evening, people were still up and about. Most of them were sitting and talking in groups in various yards and gardens of the people who lived there. The population of Ferdinandshof at that time must have been four or five times its original size.

We joined one group of several dozen people and families who were seated on a lawn. It did not take us very long to find out why there were so many people in the village. Just outside of Ferdinandshof toward the east stood a large forest, through which led the only road one could take to get beyond it. The Russian army had left a large contingent of Mongol soldiers in this forest, who had set up camps there. They were apparently not allowed to enter any of the villages but had been told that the forest area was theirs to do in what they wanted. The result was that any travellers who crossed through this forest became their prey. Several people who had dared to try to cross the forest had horror stories to tell of what went on in there. They had barely saved their lives, unlike others who had not been so lucky. Now everyone had become fearful and because the wooded area was so large there was just no other way around to get to the east, and more and more people became stranded here. They all told of experiences similar to what we had been through; very few still owned a horse, while hundreds, like ourselves, had to travel on foot, if they could travel at all.

The Russian army had also set up some kind of headquarters in the village, which they called the Russian *Commandantur*. One officer was in charge and apparently tried his best to keep his army under control. Rumour had it that the soldiers by now had orders to leave the German population alone. Nevertheless, it still happened frequently that people were robbed, as we could attest, and that women were raped. The garden in which we sat down was located toward the end of the village. Suddenly there appeared six or seven Russian soldiers, all in dirty uniforms and with definite Mongolian facial characteristics. They pointed their machine guns at us and began to search through everyone's belongings. One of them came towards my mother and me. With a knife he slit open one of our bags and found a felt hat which was one of the useless things that had not found a taker until now, and which I had kept. He wanted that hat but since I was frozen with fear and did not hand it to him right away, he set his bayonet on my chest and yelled something at me. He then bent down and took the hat himself and walked away. All this had not taken more than a few minutes, but it was more than any of us could stand any longer. We all grabbed what they had left us and walked into the centre of the village where most people had congregated.

It now began to get darker and we needed a place to sleep. My mother and I followed some fifty or so people who had been in Ferdinandshof already for several days, climbing up a tall ladder into the hay loft of a barn. It was at least 20 feet high above the floor. Some of the men tied up about ten horses in the space below us, then climbed up into the loft as well and pulled the ladder up behind them. In this way we spent the night, just as we had been used to doing in Thurow.

The next morning I walked back twice to the wagon that we had abandoned the previous day and salvaged some of our stuff that I thought might be of some use. There were the old curtains we had found in a destroyed house, a zinc wash basin, two cooking pots and similar items, but most importantly the sugar beet pail with the golden watch in it. I asked the woman in whose hayloft we slept whether I could store some of our things in her attic and she gave me permission to do so. She commented that a great many people already had done the same and that our few things would not make a difference. I did tell her though, that I would come back for our belongings once things had gotten back to normal.

During the nights that followed we often heard screaming and shouting and shooting, but nobody dared to move or make any sound at all. On one of the nights, however, it must have been the fourth or fifth, we heard some commotion outside in the yard. Suddenly the barn door was kicked open and several drunken soldiers entered, singing and yelling. The horses became nervous, while we barely dared to breathe. One of the women, however, lost her nerves. She suddenly began to shriek that she could stand it no longer and was going to leave. With that she ran to the edge of the loft and fell head over heels among the startled horses. She cried out for help but just at that moment we heard more Russians entering the barn, and a commanding Russian voice. Obviously the officer in charge had been notified and had sent a patrol to establish order. The people who owned the barn had been awakened, and came out and took care of the injured woman, who, we later heard, had broken an arm and one leg.

The stories that the different people told were all filled with similar tragedies. They all lost practically everything they ever owned, many had been beaten or raped, all had been plundered numerous times. The sister of one of the women we talked to had been nailed to a barn door because she had put up some resistance.

My mother and I realized of course that we could not stay there indefinitely. The only place we could remotely call home now, was Thurow. I did not like the idea at all of returning there once more but we really did not have any other place to go. At that time it did not yet occur to us that we would have to start our lives all over again in a strange place. We still believed that we would be able to return to Brietzig eventually, even if we had to wait a few more weeks. The immediate question was, how could we get back to Thurow? Most of the other people to whom we talked wanted to wait it out. They figured that the Mongolian hordes could not stay forever in the forest and they hoped to be able to return to their original homes some time soon.

Rumours of what was happening in the rest of Germany were now getting plentiful. Some things were certain by now: Hitler was dead, Germany was completely crushed and the country now apparently had been divided into two parts, the east and the west. One of the rumours was that all people who had stayed at home in the eastern part of the country were by now either dead or had been transported by the Russians to Siberia for slave labour. Villages and towns were said to have been bombed or burned to the ground. I believed that there must have been some truth to these stories, judging by what we had experienced ourselves. Therefore it just did not seem a wise thing to try to return to Brietzig at this time, especially since we would then be even further east, and further away from what now had become known as the "western zone", which was governed by the Americans.

I felt this was where we should go, if there was no hope of ever returning home. My mother did not completely agree with me. She found the idea of never being able to go back home unthinkable. However, we agreed, that for the time being we needed to go back to Thurow. Other rumours about all kinds of things were still rampant. One of them was that maybe trains would be reinstalled soon, which would help solve our problem. From then on I went every day to the local train station to inquire about any news in this regard.

After about a week, there actually appeared a train one day. Immediately it was mobbed and within a few minutes was filled to over-capacity. It was headed for Berlin. My mother and I did not manage to get on it.

From that day on, a train ran once a day and if people wanted to get on it they had to buy train tickets. We had some money left, so I purchased two tickets. I can't exactly remember which way the train went, but we did end up in Anklam, the largest town near Thurow. We were lucky; the little narrow gauge train was still in operation and with it we again arrived in Thurow, once more with only what we could carry. We had transferred the watch and our remaining money into a smaller jar of syrup and had again taken it with us.

In Thurow for the Third Time

MY FEAR THAT THE PEOPLE IN THUROW would tease us and laugh at us for having failed in our attempt to reach home was unfounded. With the exception of the Krose family, they all were very understanding and accepted us back.

Again we moved back into the gable room in the old schoolhouse. The furniture consisted of a single bed, a table and two chairs. There was no closet, but it had a *Kachelofen*, which is a built-in tile hearth that stood from the floor up to a foot below the ceiling. It had two openings at the bottom, one with a grid for the wood or coal to be burned and one below to catch the ashes. Halfway up was a third opening that was used to keep things warm. Each of these openings had an iron door in front of it. Since there was no other cooking facility we had to cook in this hearth by placing a pot with a lid directly on the burning wood or by placing it on the grid and using the ash opening as a fire station. Every day the room was filled with smoke which made it especially hard for my mother, who did most of the cooking. It aggravated her asthma. In the summer we could open the door and the window, but during the winter months it was terrible.

We had been away from Thurow about two weeks, but during that time some things had changed. In the neighbouring village of Spantekow, which was about three or four kilometres away, a new mayor had been appointed. He was a German man, but was very friendly with the Russians, probably to his benefit. Spantekow was the largest village in the area and he had been placed in charge of it and the smaller surrounding villages, to which Thurow also belonged. One day shortly after we had returned, he appeared in Thurow with two Russian soldiers and sent a messenger around for everyone to come out to meet him. There were about 60 German people in the whole village and then the 40 or so Russian soldiers in the main house. He declared that from now on we all had to work in the fields and that the "Soll" had to be fulfilled.

This meant that every village, according to its population, had to deliver a weekly percentage of the produce they were harvesting to him in Spantekow and he, in turn, would deliver it to the Russian army. This man—his name was Stark—of course knew Mr. Krose and Leu and Benzin, but he did not want any of them to be in charge in Thurow. He probably was afraid they might outsmart him. He looked at me, and knowing that I was the youngest and had not been there more than a year, appointed me to be the new Mayor of Thurow. I am sure he imagined that I would be easily manipulated and would follow his orders.

So here I was with all the responsibility to keep the farm going with eight old horses and a few people. Each Saturday we had to load up a wagon filled with potatoes, grain and other produce and drive it to Spantekow. From the beginning I kept the amounts to a minimum and explained to Stark that there just was not any more. This was not true; we had had a very good harvest the year before and I knew where the foodstuff for the village was preserved and we kept most of it.

Each person in the village now had to work for the "common good", which meant women and children also had to work in the fields. I had neither the power nor intention to order anybody around. The men who had returned just recently from their time in prison recognized the seriousness of the situation, and all, except for Ernst Krose, helped me to get a daily work crew going. Naturally, all of us also realized that we had to bring the harvest in this fall if we wanted any guarantee of surviving the coming winter. It was a blessing that due to the foresight of Mr. Krose the crops had been sown in the spring before we left with our trek. My job still was to get up at 3 o'clock in the morning to feed the horses.

By August, some of the men and I had been fortunate enough to recapture some of the cows that had wandered loose in the meadows. We had returned about 10 of them back to the main barn. Each morning, after the horses were fed, the cows had to be milked and fed as well. By six o'clock I had milked three of them, the men milked the others. One man then divided the milk out to the families in the village, so that everyone had their fair share. I always took my portion with me right away before I went for breakfast, which mostly consisted of hot, crushed barley or oat grain with milk or boiled potatoes and milk. Since there was no bakery in the village we did not have bread for a very long time. Even though we tried to grind flour and bake some bread ourselves it did not turn out very palatable. I did, however, make our own butter in an old butter churn that I found in the attic. Generally speaking, we were much better off than people who lived in the cities.

My job as "mayor" included the keeping of some records of the daily work that was done, how many people had been involved, how much was harvested and how much was delivered to the Russian army. It always had to be one half of what we had gained. Of course, my amounts were always lower than they actually should have been.

Juergen Returns

OUR LITTLE TRAIN WAS STILL RUNNING twice every week to Anklam and back. One day, at the beginning of October, 1945, I boarded it. The reason for this trip I cannot remember. On the way back, shortly after the train had left the station in Anklam, I noticed a woman sitting not far from me who looked quite familiar. After a second glance it suddenly dawned on me that it was Tante Else from Berlin, my father's older sister. I had not seen her for several years and the thought went through my head: "What in the world is she doing here in this godforsaken place?" I jumped up, hugged and welcomed her and we both began to cry. I had a million questions and so probably had she.

Some mail delivery had again started by the end of August and my mother and I had written to her, in the hope she still might have survived at her former address in Berlin, letting her know that the two of us were still in Thurow. We had, though, never received an answer from her and now, all of a sudden, she was here on this train!

After the first excitement she pushed me away and said: "Don't you want to say 'hello' to your brother?" At first I didn't realize what she meant, but then my eyes fell on the skeleton of a young man sitting beside her and after a few seconds of shock I recognized the features of my brother, Juergen.

His 16-year-old face was dominated by two very big blue eyes, a long pointed nose and cheekbones sticking out from under his skin that was as white as a sheet. His hair showed white strands at the temples and beside him leaned two crutches.

This was one of the happy moments in my life where all the suffering and tribulation was forgotten. All three of us cried for joy and happiness, having found each other again. The real ecstasy came, however, when we arrived in Thurow and met my mother. She could not believe what she saw when the three of us stood in front of the door. For a moment she seemed to have been frozen but then a flood of joyful tears broke forth and we all joined in again.

Due to the fact that we had food to eat, we tried to feed Juergen and Tante Else royally with milk and potato soup, and potato pancakes fried in butter. We now even had some bread left from a loaf I was able to bring back every Saturday from the bakery in Spantekow. The baker's daughter, with whom I had struck up a friendship, handed me one loaf secretly every week. Bread still tasted better than cake to us. The result of our exaggerated hospitality was that Juergen became violently ill. He had been on starvation rations for so long that his body could not deal with the sudden gluttony. But after several days of "TLC", he recuperated. Tante Else stayed with us for about a week in the little attic room, that now four of us shared. Juergen and I slept on the floor, Tante Else and our mother shared the bed.

•

JUERGEN'S STORY BEGAN AT CHRISTMAS of 1944, when our family— our parents and the two of us—were at home in Brietzig for one last time. Our father instructed all of us at that time to contact his sister Else in Berlin should we ever become separated from one another. We memorized her address: Heinrich Rollerstr. 20, Berlin-Weissensee. It seemed unthinkable that Berlin would ever be in real danger, other than from air attacks.

At age 16, Juergen left in January 1945 for Bavaria, where he had been drafted into a training camp. This was the last information we had had as to his whereabouts. What we did not know was that he had been sent to the front line around Berlin as the war neared its end, and together with other young boys of the same age, had to help defend Berlin.

Now, back in Thurow, Juergen was very reluctant to tell us anything about these days of man-to-man fighting, and to this day he does not want to discuss that time in his life. We did find out a few details, though.

He had been involved in a battle at Koenigswusterhausen near Berlin where he received a serious knee injury. The shot had gone through his right knee, in one side and out the other. Of course, he could not fight anymore and was placed into the war hospital in Koenigswusterhausen, which on that day, was still in German hands. However, on the following day, the Russian front moved forward and the town, including the hospital, became occupied by the Russians.

Juergen said a group of Russian soldiers entered the hospital, went through the wards and shot every third German soldier in his bed. He happened to be number two. From then on, most beds were used for wounded Russian soldiers and most German soldiers were booted out. The German doctors and nurses had to tend first to the wounded Russians. Juergen told us that one nurse—I have forgotten whether she was German or Russian—had pity on him. She discovered that his bandage hadn't been changed for days. The wound had become badly infected and lice and maggots began to crawl around under the bandage. Apparently, Juergen was scheduled for a leg amputation, but partly due to the fact that the maggots cleaned his wound and partly to this nurse's care, who began changing the dressing from time to time, it never came to this. After several months Juergen was given a pair of crutches and he began to learn to walk again.

One day in September, Juergen was allowed for the first time to take a walk outside in the hospital grounds. He discovered that it was located alongside a fairly busy street. On one of his next walks a few days later, he threw a note which he had scribbled on a piece of paper over the fence onto the adjacent sidewalk. It contained a message and a plea for help to Tante Else with her address. He had also begged the person who would find this note to deliver it to Tante Else. It so happened that a woman came along who saw the note being tossed over the fence. She picked it up, read it and, bless her heart, delivered it to Tante Else who in turn spared no inconvenience to try to get permission to visit Juergen. She pretended to be his mother and after several unsuccessful attempts, she finally was allowed to visit him. A few weeks later, Juergen was dismissed into her care and stayed in her apartment for about a week, after which she brought him to us in Thurow. After a few weeks of motherly care, Juergen had sufficiently recuperated to do some easy chores in the stables and in the field.

CHAPTER SEVEN

Becoming a Landowner

Things had changed in the village during the month of September. The Russian *Commandanture* had decided that every large farm, such as the one in Thurow, would henceforth no longer exist but would be divided up into small parcels. These were to be given to the workers who had been living in the village, and who now were to become farmers in their own right. The purpose behind this decision was undoubtedly the fact that direct demands could be made of individuals who were personally responsible for their produce.

Later, when the small property owners could no longer fulfill the demanded obligations because they had neither horses nor machines, the land would be turned into *Kolchosen*, or state ownership.

For now, each new "farmer" had to deliver a percentage of goods to a collection place for the Russian army. The registrar's office in Anklam was approached and Mr. Krose's farm was divided up into as many parts as there were families. I was one of the recipients and still have the document to show that I became the owner of a farm of 20 hectares—about 50 acres. A stretch of bush was part of my land.

Since there were only a few horses left, lots were drawn for them. My mother had picked the lot for me and, voilà, she had drawn the strongest of all the horses for me. I still remember its name, it was Lotte; I had had my eye on her all along. Of all the horses that were left, she still was in the best condition.

The new owners now had to look after the animals themselves, but they also had to share them with the people who had not been lucky enough to get one. The work had to be done jointly. There was also one tractor that was still working, and some machinery that had been in use the year before.

The few cows that were left were divided up in the same manner, but we were not lucky enough this time to get one. However, it was not too long thereafter and I managed to acquire a cow for ourselves. This happened in the following manner.

Throughout the summer, the Russians had collected all the herds they could find in stables or meadows and driven them on foot to the closest larger train stations where they loaded them into box cars and transported them eastward to Russia. We had seen several herds of cows and sheep coming through our village, a few hundred at a time, guarded by armed soldiers in the front and the rear. The schoolhouse in which my mother and I, and now also Juergen, lived in one room lay at the corner of a bend in the road. It had a wooden fence around the yard and several small rooms in a larger barn in which the former teacher had kept some sheep and pigs and probably a cow as well. I had cleaned these stalls out and moved some foodstuff—potatoes, carrots and grain—into them for our own use, which I had recovered from the main barns on the farm property.

In anticipation of another herd of animals coming through, I had collected a large pile of turnips and sugar beets with the leaves still in place and stored them as well. When one day I saw a herd of cows approaching, I ran into my little barn, grabbed an armful of sugar beet leaves and spread them from the road across our yard into the open barn. Sure enough, one of the cows followed the food train and ate her way into our barn. The soldiers in the front had just passed our house when this happened and the end of the herd was still beyond the bend so the soldiers in the back could not see what went on in the front. As fast as I could I closed the door shut behind the cow, gave her some more to eat and danced and laughed for joy, having a cow and having fooled those darn Russians.

I used the same method to catch two sheep a few days later. Since we had not eaten any meat for months, one of the men in the village killed one of the sheep for us and I gave him the second for his family to eat. For the next weeks and months we ate salted mutton each week a few times. To this day I cannot stand the taste of lamb or mutton.

As it turned out, we were indeed very fortunate, since the cow happened to be pregnant and not long after we had her, she delivered a calf. From then on we had lots of milk. I found an old centrifuge in our attic, which we used to separate the cream from the rest of the milk. I was also able to organize an old butter churn so now we had lots of butter and milk, more than we could use ourselves. At that time people in the cities had very little to eat. What could be bought for food stamps was very meager and the lines in front of stores were huge. Almost daily, people came from Anklam and other nearby places into the villages and went from door to door trying to trade commodities for food. In this way, by trading milk and butter, we acquired some bedding, a few blankets, some dishes and cutlery and other household items. After a few weeks we sold the calf to another family in the village.

Russian Soldiers in our German Village

THE SOLDIERS WHO LIVED IN THE MANSION had not bothered us too much. They seemed to be quite self-sufficient, probably getting their food and necessities delivered from some depot. Every so often we saw them arriving in the village in carriages with girls at their sides, mostly on weekends. We always heard loud music, shouting and goings-on at the main house, but mostly they left us in peace. There were a few exceptions.

One afternoon in early November, when I was doing the books downstairs in the old schoolhouse, two drunken soldiers suddenly burst through the door. They each swung an open bottle of vodka in their hands, plunked themselves onto a bench and motioned for me to drink with them. They became so insistent that I had to take a sip, which tasted horrible. When they did not stop urging me to drink, I just put the bottle beside my mouth and let the stuff run down my blouse. They were far enough gone not to realize what I did and when the bottles were empty, they mumbled something in German about coming back and staggered out the door.

I had become very scared, ran upstairs and changed, and did not go down again for fear they might return. I do not remember where our mother was on this evening, but she definitely was not in our room, though Juergen was. I told him what had happened and the two of us pushed as much furniture as we could in front of the door. A chair stood underneath the doorknob and the table and some shelves were barricading the door.

We hoped that nothing would happen, but around eight o'clock when it was dark already, we heard some commotion downstairs and then someone came tramping up the stairs. Then followed heavy banging on the door and a voice shouting, *"Frau raus, Frau raus!"* (Woman, out!).

I was frozen with fear but Juergen had his wits about him. He realized that sooner or later the soldier would break the door down, so he very quickly tied several bed sheets together, then told me to climb out of the window and slide down while he held one end of it. I had to jump the last five or six feet and remember falling pretty hard on the ground, then felt the bed sheets falling on top of me. As I got up and grabbed the sheets I could hear the door crashing upstairs and the soldier yelling, *"Wo Frau, wo Frau?"* I did not wait to hear Juergen's answer but ran with my bed sheets as fast as I could in the dark to the nearest ditch behind the village, where I stayed until I saw the light go out in our room.

Eventually I crept as silently as I could to the house at the end of the village, where another young girl lived with her parents. They took me in for the night. Poor Juergen had to suffer some punches and kicks from those two drunken soldiers because they hadn't found me, and he had said he did not know where I was.

Harvest Time 1945

IN SEPTEMBER AND OCTOBER the harvest was in full swing. Most of my days I spent on the tractor, pulling the grain cutting machine and helping the few men bring in the rye, wheat, oats and barley. I was up at 3:00 a.m. to feed the horses, milk the cows, had breakfast around 6:00, to the fields at 7:00, and to bed at 9:00 p.m. On Saturdays, I got no sleep at all because that was the night of the dance in the next village of Nerdin, and I had no intention of missing one.

One day, when I was riding the tractor fairly close to one of the few dirt roads, one of the wheels suddenly sank into a hole and got stuck. Two of the village men who were with me in the field and I pushed the vehicle out and wondered what could have caused the hole. We started to dig and found the remains of a Russian soldier in his uniform buried in a shallow grave. As fast as we could we covered him up again and agreed not to tell anybody about our find.

Of course we speculated how and why he might have gotten there. We suddenly remembered having seen a carriage with four soldiers racing through the village about two or three weeks prior. As two of the soldiers held on to a third one between them, to keep him from falling over, they had left in the direction of this field. We had presumed he was drunk, as they usually were, and had not given it a further thought. Now we came to the conclusion that he must have been dead already and that they just had gotten rid of him. We never did say anything and nothing ever came of it.

Once the harvest was over and the weather got colder, we were ordered to go into the forest near Spantekow and cut down trees. By this time, Juergen had regained his strength and for weeks on end we would be driven each day on an open truck, together with the other men and women from the village, into the forest. Juergen and I always tried to stay close together and work in the same area. These tough times drew us closer together than ever and we established a bond of belonging together that has lasted throughout our lives.

Those years in Thurow, especially 1945-46, were by far the ones I worked the hardest physically. But it was strange for me to notice that the harder I worked, the stronger I seemed to become. Today I know that it is part of one of the laws of the universe. The hard work did not seem to bother me too much, except that I kept on thinking: "This is not what I want to do for the rest of my life. Somehow, there must be a way out of this."

By this time the Krose family had left Thurow. They were just gone one day and no one knew or much cared where or why they went. After my mother and I had returned from our unsuccessful trip to Brietzig, they had not talked to me anymore because they considered me to be a traitor. They held it against me that I had not supported them when they tried to move back into the mansion, and that I had not protested on their behalf when the Russian *Commandanture* divided the farm up into small parcels, but had myself accepted a piece of land. I did not care at that time anymore. Times had changed. I had to keep my mother, my brother and myself alive and all the protesting in the world would not have resulted in them getting their farm back. I also felt that they looked at all of us in the village as their serfs, and I certainly was not to be some-one's slave.

Both Leu and Benzin had left the village as well. Benzin had found his family somewhere, and Leu's family lived in Anklam. His father and brother owned a nursery in Anklam and he had gone back to help.

In Thurow there were a few young people, Juergen's and my age, which we came to know quite well. As time went on, life got somewhat back to "normal". Every Saturday night there was a dance at the Inn in Nerdin, about two or three kilometres east of Thurow. Though we all worked very hard six days a week, on Saturday evening after work we would walk as a group, about 10 or 12 of us, to the dance. The band played all through the night until 5 a.m. and we would stay until the last dance, and I did not sit out a single dance all night. It was the one bright light for all of us and I wished I could be a professional dancer. On Sunday morning I just went to our room to change and then immediately back into the barns to tend to the horses and cows. The rest of the day I would catch up on lost sleep and start the routine on Monday morning all over again.

During one of the Saturday dances I met a young man who was about two or three years older than I. He had just returned home from the army and he was a terrific dancer. He probably thought that of me, too, because soon we were dancing together all the time. It did not take very long before I fell in love with him and he liked me too. After the dance was over he began to walk me home, even though he lived in Krien, which was in the opposite direction of Thurow. We parted with a goodbye kiss and waited for the next Saturday. His name was Ulrich Papke. We never met at any other time or at any other place, only in Nerdin at the dance, and we walked back to Thurow with the rest of the group.

Leu

SOMETIMES ON A SUNDAY AFTERNOON Leu would come from Anklam to visit. He always came on his bicycle. One weekend in the late fall, he and I drove in a buggy with my horse to Ferdinandshof. I had told him that my mother and I had left several of our belongings in the attic of one of the farmhouses and he offered to come along and help me to retrieve them.

The weather was beautiful that weekend; we had a wonderful ride and I enjoyed getting out of Thurow, experiencing a bit of freedom. We arrived in Ferdinandshof in the late afternoon without having been stopped or being molested by roving soldiers. When I requested to get my things from the attic, the farmer's wife declared that none of the things in her attic were there any more and she would not let us in. I became quite upset. Those old pots and towels and things seemed like a valuable treasure which was mine, and I needed it back.

Leu suggested we call the police. The village had one "gendarme" who willingly came with us and demanded that we be let in. As the woman had said, there was nothing left in the attic except a few curtain pieces strewn over the floor and a few rags that could have been towels at one time. I asked the policeman to let me go through the house to see whether she had something in her rooms that belonged to me, and sure enough, I found a few of my belongings, including two small tablecloths, a few towels and some kitchenware.

I am sure she had thought that none of the refugees whose things she had stored in her attic would ever return to claim them, so she had taken what she liked and used it herself. I collected what I could find, about half of the things we had left behind a few months earlier. We had some money with us and rented two rooms in a local inn, then started on our way home the next morning.

I had noticed all along that Leu liked me, and at one of his Sunday visits he asked me to marry him. I was quite surprised about this quick development and really did not like him all that much. He was tall and lanky, had a lot of acne on his face, and sometimes used language that I didn't like and that made me feel embarrassed. On the other hand he was very friendly and quite nice to me. I told him I had to think about it and besides he had to ask my mother for my hand in marriage, since my father had not returned from the war. I thought that was quite the romantic way to do it and besides, it would give me a second opinion.

During the following days I did a lot of thinking about this proposal, my train of thought was one of logic, not of love. What attracted me was the fact that his brother owned this nursery and he worked there, which meant that he had an income and a place to live in the family home. I visited that house once and found it to be quite roomy and, for those times, the family seemed to be quite well-off. They were an old established family who had lived there for generations and during the war had not lost all that much. I figured that if I married him, my mother could come with me and would be taken care of and I could get my grandfather, Hildebrandt, whom I adored, to live with us and make his last years easier. He lived in Berlin with his youngest daughter Marianne, my mother's sister, her husband, three young children and Marianne's father-in-law, in two rooms. According to my estimation, it would be a step up for all of us and our future would be more secure than it was at the moment.

On New Year's Eve, 1945, Leu came again to visit me and to officially ask my mother for her blessing. I was extremely nervous and did not know whether to hope for her to say yes or no. She was caught by surprise since I had not prepared her. Leu had arrived in the afternoon, it must have been around 4 p.m. when he came upstairs. I remember that it was almost dark in the room, he stood by the door, my mother was close to the window and I stood somewhere in between the two. My mother was quite shocked, although I suspect that she had seen it coming. She told him that I was still too young, not even 21 (which I would be in four weeks' time), and that she could not make this decision without my father for whose return we were still waiting.

Leu responded with all kinds of promises for the future and asked me to come over to him, since we did not really need the permission of my mother. I did not move and the conversation went on for 10 or 15 minutes. Finally my mother announced a definite "No" as far as she was concerned, and asked me whose side I was on.

I had not said anything the whole time, but when she put the decision to me, which I interpreted as it being either she or him, I went over to her. Without saying another word, Leu turned and left the room. That was the last time I ever saw him. And to this day I am grateful to my mother for having refused to let me make this terrible mistake, and for not saying, "You do what you please." At the time I loved Ulli Papke, but I had seriously considered marrying Leu for the sake of what I thought would have been a secure future for the rest of my family.

Winter, 1945-46

THOSE WINTER MONTHS, especially January and February 1946, were dreadful. We were three adults living in that one small room without a stove to cook on. There was just the tiled stove, the smoke filling the room constantly and my mother was always ill with asthma. The room was cold and drafty. By the end of January the work in the forest stopped because there was too much snow and Juergen and I had nothing to do all day long except feeding the animals. All three of us became more and more restless and despondent. We would sit every evening making plans of how to get out of Thurow and what we could do with the rest of our lives. Even the weekly dances in Nerdin did not compensate for the unhappiness that we felt.

During these weeks our mother received a letter from Walter Mehlberg who had been a farmer in Kossin, the neighbouring village of Brietzig. He informed her of the fate of our father.

The two of them had been in Siberia together in a POW camp and he had just returned from there, while our father had been held back. Apparently our father had developed dropsy, his face was swollen with water and he, too, had been scheduled to be sent home. However, he had washed and mended his clothes, had a haircut and looked well fed because of the swelling of his face. At the last moment he was pulled back and had to remain because he looked too healthy and well. Besides, he was needed in a mine as an expert electrician and was kept in the camp. As sad and despondent as this new tragedy was for my brother and for me, the new heartache must have been devastating for our poor mother, who bravely tried to hide her anguish, sorrow and worry from us.

Later on, Mehlberg visited our mother and told her details about their prisoners' life in Siberia, and still later, Frieda Hinz, our babysitter in Brietzig, returned from the same camp and gave us more information. Our father never returned. He died of a broken heart in Protopovsk, not far from Lake Baikal in Siberia, we think at the end of 1945.

By the end of February 1946, rumors began to circulate that several young people from neighbouring villages had been drafted to work in some factories in Demmin and Stettin. There was talk that all young people under the age of 25 would be sent to some factories that the Russians had opened. This was the absolute last thing we were willing to do and we decided to leave Thurow as soon as possible, come what may.

CHAPTER EIGHT

We Break for the Black Border

We knew that the longer we waited, the worse the situation would become, and the less chance we might have to leave.

During the summer I had become friends with a girl, Gerda, who was two years older than I. She was the daughter of the former teacher in the village of Spantekow and she and her mother had left in late fall to stay with relatives in the city of Helmstedt in West Germany. They had crossed the so-called "black border", and now I was receiving letters from Gerda telling me to join her in Helmstedt.

The rumour mill was in high gear about what would happen in the Russian Zone versus how good it was in the American Zone, and how difficult and dangerous it was to cross the border. Apparently the border between East and West Germany was patrolled on the east side by armed guards, parts of the border was closed off with electrical wires, and any *Grenzgaenger* (border crossers), when caught by the Russians, would be punished terribly.

The result of all this talk was that fear was spreading and people were very reluctant to chance leaving the Russian Zone. We took all this into consideration, but Gerda had written to me that they had made it without having been caught. Thank goodness, at that time the letters were not yet being censored as they were later. She had informed me that they had taken a train to Magdeburg, near the border, where she had managed to acquire a Red Cross nurse's outfit. She and her mother had then waited for the next refugee train, which came through daily from Selesia and Pommerania, each containing more than 1,000 expelled Germans in freight cars. The two women were taken into the Red Cross freight car with the sick and thus crossed the border. Once in West Germany, she had found work as a Red Cross nurse in a refugee camp near Helmstedt and she assured me that there would be enough work for me as well.

Juergen's and my mood had become gloomier and gloomier as the winter went on, and by the beginning of March we were ready to dare just about anything. So with our mother's consent we made the decision to leave. We debated long hours about how to do it and how we could take our mother with us. But it was she who insisted that she remain behind. She felt that our chances with her would be limited because we were young and could run fast while she would hold us back. Eventually we gave in, but promised to get her out of Thurow as soon as we had found a foothold on the other side of the border.

Our decision was finally made. We would leave, come what may, for better or worse. However, in order to leave we needed an official permit to buy a train ticket.[1]

The plan we hatched and carried out was as follows: I would go to see Stark—the Russian-appointed overseer—in Spantekow, of whom I had the lowest possible opinion. He not only was a traitor in our eyes, he also was unbelievably stupid. His spoken and written messages were full of grammatical and spelling mistakes and usually made no sense at all. He was also conceited and overbearing, and I knew that I could get to him through flattery.

So I made an appointment. I complimented him on his organizational skills and then laid out the future possibilities for Thurow if there were a university-trained agriculturist available to help him plan strategies, not only for Thurow, but for the neighbouring villages as well. I of-

---

1   Permits were required for virtually everything at this time in Germany. Even as "Mayor" of Thurow, I had to have an official permit just to use the bicycle which had been especially assigned to me. This permit, both in Russian and German, is still in my possession.

fered that I was willing to take this training at the university in Rostock.

Attending that university had always been my plan even before the war ended. Now, however, I had no idea whether it, or any other university in the country, had reopened again. I doubted it very much.

As I suspected, Stark did not know anything about universities and took my word for it. He was very impressed with my idea and seemed to anticipate his own possible advantage at my suggestion, so he agreed quickly to my plan.

I explained I had to get to Rostock somehow, and that the distance was far too great to even think of riding my bike there. So I requested two train permits to Rostock, via Helmstedt, one for myself and one for my brother, who had to accompany me to help carry my suitcases, of which I had none. Stark fell for the ruse.

Because he was so ignorant of local geography, he did not realize that Rostock, which lay in the Russian Zone, could never be reached by way of Helmstedt, which was located in the American-controlled zone. Rather than complicate things, the permit he magnanimously agreed to fill out did not specify a final destination. He was letting me know how much power he had, and how important he was, while I silently rejoiced.

I carried the permit home like a trophy; the first step had been successful! Juergen and I each packed a backpack with a few belongings, a change of clothes, a towel, soap and toothbrush (we used soap to brush our teeth), a set of cutlery, cup and plate, a blanket each and whatever we had to eat. I remember a piece of bread and a jar of sugar beet syrup.

We left on the morning of March 17, 1946. Our little train took us to Anklam. No permit was necessary for this stretch. It must have been terrible for our mother to let us go, not knowing where we would end up or what dangers we might encounter. All my life I have been grateful to her for having had the faith in us and trusting us to find a way to a better life than Thurow would ever have to offer.

In Anklam, we showed our permit at the ticket booth and bought a ticket to Berlin. I do not remember how much money we each had, but I do remember that we had acquired some in earlier months by selling butter and milk. The train ride from Anklam to Berlin went without interruption and was uneventful. We arrived some time in the afternoon and attempted to buy tickets to Magdeburg. After having waited for a very long time in a long line, we were told that no train would leave for Magdeburg any more on that day and we should try again the following day.

Instead of spending the night at the overcrowded train station we decided to look up our mother's younger sister, Marianne. I had mentioned earlier in what conditions she and her family lived, but we felt we would like to say goodbye to them, and mainly to our grandfather, whom both of us loved.

They were happy to see us and let us sleep in their small kitchen on the floor. Just before the end of the war they all had been evacuated from their spacious home in Berlin-Tegel. Marianne, the three children and the two old men had been sent to Triebsees near Stralsund by the Baltic Sea to be safe from the air attacks on Berlin. There they experienced the end of the war and all the horrors of it. Marianne had been raped frequently, once by several Russians in front of her children.

After the end of the war, they had trekked back to Berlin, mostly on foot. My grandfather, who was then in his 70s, had been separated from the rest of the family and walked the whole distance. They reunited in Berlin but soon were ordered to leave their old apartment, and were given the two rooms in which we now found them.

Our grandfather accompanied us the following day to the train station, and did so again on the following two days before we were able to actually buy a ticket for a train bound for Magdeburg. Each day, there were hundreds and hundreds of people crowding the ticket wicket, and we just could not come close. On the third day we had left in the middle of the night and finally were able to buy two tickets. Again we were requested to show our permit and I was grateful that Stark had filled it out without giving the destination as Rostock. It was simply a permit to use the train.

We left that morning and it was the last time we ever saw our grandfather. He must have sensed it; it was a very sad departure.

Crossing the Black Border

JUERGEN AND I WERE LUCKY. When the train arrived, a door stopped just in front of us and we both got a seat by the window. People crowded in and when the train started to move, there was not even standing room left. For about 20 minutes everything went fine and nobody complained. Then the train stopped in Potsdam. We could see at once that the whole platform, as far as it went, was filled with Russian soldiers.

The moment the train stopped they all piled in, yelling and screaming and pushing the German passengers out of the opposite doors onto the tracks. Those that lingered or did not move fast enough were hit with guns and pistols. Of course Juergen and I had to jump out as well. I would not have known what to do, but Juergen grabbed my hand and pulled me to one of the permanently fastened ladders on the coaches. He climbed up onto the roof of the train and I followed close behind.

By now I saw everyone doing the same thing. In no time at all the roofs of all coaches were covered with bodies lying on their stomachs, holding on to the edges of the coaches. All this had happened within minutes. As soon as all the Russians were in the train, it took off again, leaving many of the passengers, who had started in Berlin, behind.

Soon thereafter it began to rain.

We had our knapsacks on our backs. Like everyone else, we lay on our stomachs and held on for dear life to whatever there was to hold on to. To this day I am still surprised that we did not fall off. We lay there for hours on end, through forests and tunnels, and all the while it rained. Normally it would have been a four-hour ride, but the train stopped in many places and more people climbed onto the roofs.

I cannot remember exactly how long it took before the train finally rolled into the station in Magdeburg. It was dark, we were soaked to the skin, stiff from the position we had been in for hours, tired, hungry, angry, frustrated and fearful. However, we were also glad that we had gotten thus far without major harassment and that we still had each other.

Juergen seemed less fearful than I was; if not, he pretended to be, which in turn gave me some of my courage back. We spent the night in the crowded waiting room at the Magdeburg station, tried to dry up somewhat and listened to the conversations of the people around us. It did not take long to realize that the border was not too far away, and that there were always so-called *Grenzgaenger*, men who you could hire to take you across the border. However, we did not have enough money to hire some one like that, and Juergen was not convinced that that would be the best idea anyway. He thought that you could not really trust anyone at this time. Some of these guys might sell their "clients" over to the Russians and play both sides.

We decided to follow my friend Gerda's suggestions and try to get on one of the refugee trains that crossed over every day. These trains always consisted of only freight cars in which people were transported. Since they came from the German provinces that had been signed over to Poland after the war ended, they were always accompanied by Polish soldiers. We heard that the next train was expected at around six o'clock in the morning, and sure enough, it arrived.

Juergen and I had been hiding behind a parked train and watched the refugee train arrive and stop. We saw Polish soldiers leave the car behind the locomotive and noticed that others were positioned in the last car of the train. The car with the sign of the Red Cross was the second behind the locomotive, too close to the soldiers. Once those that left the train had passed by us, we dashed to a car that had the big door rolled back and people were looking out. We tried to climb in as fast as we could, but the German refugees were just as frightened as we were, and did not want to let us in. They shouted they had been counted and there was a list of all of their names and if two more people showed up they all would get into trouble, and two would certainly be shot.

All this talk caused some commotion and made the soldiers turn around and come back to investigate. The people on the train pointed the two of us out and told them that we were trying to get on. The Polish soldiers were stern, though not altogether unfriendly. They ordered us back out again, took us by the arm to the front of the train and made us climb into the car that they had just left. Some of these men spoke German and started a conversation with us, asking where we came from and where we wanted to go. The train had started up again and both of us were somewhat relieved to see that they were not as terrible as the Russians.

We noticed that the train entered a heavily forested area and after a few minutes it suddenly stopped. The door was opened from the outside and we saw a group of Russian soldiers standing there. They saw us, looked at us and ordered us out immediately. We were both stunned and confused and jumped out of the opposite door which also was open. I followed Juergen, who was thinking of escape into the forest. Two of the Russians ducked under the train and caught us within a minute. They belted Juergen and pushed both of us back into the car and out on the other side. One of them pointed a machine gun at us, and pushed us ahead of him some distance into the forest until we saw a house that looked to us like a forester's house. It was not far from the train tracks. Near the house stood a train-signal hut built of stone. It was not larger than 9 by 12 feet. Into that hut he pushed us through a wooden door, which he locked shut behind us.

It took us a few seconds to adjust to the darkness inside. The room had only one tiny window in one corner. We realized that there were already about 20 people inside, and found out quickly that they, like us, had been caught in an attempt to cross the border. Some said they had been in there since the day before. All of them were very frightened. In the middle of this hut were several large signal levers, which seemed to have been out of order for some time. Some of the people had quite a bit of luggage with them. Some were sitting on boxes; most were just standing like sardines in a tin.

There were a few mothers with small children and three women with a teenaged daughter each. I was the fourth young woman in the room. One young man around our age stood in the far corner and several old men as well as a few young boys completed the sorry lot. We heard the train start again and our hopes sank another degree. The stories we heard from the people were extremely discouraging; they told of electric wires along the border and guards ready to shoot without warning, and that in some areas, field mines had been placed. The good news was that it was apparently only about half a mile from where we were now to the actual border, and once across that border there were no hidden dangers lurking. The city of Helmstedt was said to be about five kilometres past the border in a westerly direction.

When we stopped talking there was absolute silence. We could not hear any sounds from the outside. It was eerie and scary and the fear of our uncertain fate hung heavy in the air. This was another one of those days in which I learned how to pray with all the feeling and emotion I was capable of. Describing the emotions and thoughts that go through ones' mind in a situation like that is almost impossible.

All day long we sat in this little hut. There was no room for anybody to walk around—you could either sit on your luggage or stand up. In the late afternoon the door suddenly opened and a soldier with a machine gun over his shoulder entered. Since Juergen and I had been the last ones to arrive, we were sitting right next to the door on our knapsacks. The man looked around and saw me. He pulled a piece of paper out of his pocket, wrote something on it and gave it to me, indicating to put it in my pocket. I looked at the writing and saw a few Russian words and the number 11. The soldier then turned and locked the door again from the outside.

All the other people wanted to know what the note said. One old man said that he could read a bit of Russian and I showed him the paper. He told me that the words said something to the effect that he would be back at 11 and that he had marked me down for himself by signing his name beneath. This frightened me terribly; from then on I was in a state of panic. I begged the others to let me move to the far corner of the room so that I would not be the first one to be seen when he came back. They were kind enough to let Juergen and me squeeze into one corner, which happened to be where this other young man was standing. The hours passed and it got completely dark. Someone lit a candle for a while but it burned out, and we all were sitting in the dark like frightened rabbits in a cage.

Around 11 o'clock we heard several men approaching. My heart was racing so fast that I thought it would burst. Juergen pushed me down on the floor. I crouched on my arms and knees and he threw a blanket over me. Then he and the young man sat on my back, just in time before the door opened and three soldiers with a lantern stood in the door. They looked around, grabbed the three young girls, who screamed and struggled and whose mothers cried and pleaded, pulled them out the door and locked the rest of us in again.

By now everyone was in a panic. I did not feel anything anymore, I had just frozen in time. Juergen and the young man stood up again, but I stayed huddled on the floor, unable to move at all, and frightened that they might come back if they did not find the note in any of the girls' pockets. The other people seemed to have forgotten about me. Eventually Juergen pulled me up again and for a time there were no sounds but the crying of the women and children. Later we heard the faint sounds of music that were probably coming from the house, interrupted by shouts and singing. Someone began to pray and we all joined in. We prayed for the girls and for ourselves and I felt as desperate as I had months earlier when I was sitting in the rain barrel.

The hours went by, everyone had become quiet again, some people probably had dosed off. To my great relief no soldier had returned to look for me but the three girls had not been returned to us either.

Very early in the morning, it must have been between 5 and 6 o'clock, we heard loud noises outside. Cars and motorcycles seemed to arrive and there was a lot of shouting and screaming in Russian. Suddenly the door was flung open and two soldiers with their machine guns drawn motioned us to hurry out and line up. People were not allowed to take their suitcases and boxes with them, only those of us who had knapsacks quickly flung them on our backs and went outside. There was a great hurry and secrecy about this activity, we were motioned not to speak at all and walk as fast as we could in single file into the forest. Three armed soldiers accompanied us at each side. If someone stepped on a branch or made the smallest noise, they pushed the person with their guns and motioned to be quiet.

It was a chilly March morning and a light drizzling rain was falling. Our clothes had not yet dried completely from the day before, but at least we now were out in the open and not caged in anymore. We were marched into the dense forest for about half an hour, all the while being threatened to be quiet. Finally we had to stop at a clearing and were motioned to sit down. We found some logs to sit on and watched two of the guards leave while the other four positioned themselves around us with their guns ready to shoot. I picked up some mud and smeared it all over my face and my clothes, ruffed up my hair and made myself look as ugly as possible.

As the hours went by and the rain let off a little the guards relaxed somewhat and allowed us to talk quietly with one another. We had come to the conclusion that probably a control had arrived at this outpost early in the morning. We knew that by this time the Russian troops officially had been forbidden to take any more civilian prisoners or to steal or rape or harass the German population. These border guards seemed to be afraid of the authorities and had to get us out of the way as fast and quietly as possible. During the day the guards changed every few hours.

By the afternoon our group had increased to about 50 people, all persons who had been caught somewhere trying to cross the border. If one of the group had to go "behind the bushes" a soldier would go along, making sure that no one escaped. At one time Juergen started to whistle a Russian tune that he had picked up somewhere over the months, and one of the soldiers came up to him and started a conversation with him in broken German, acting in quite a friendly manner.

When it got dark, a few more soldiers arrived with flashlights. One of them seemed to be in charge. He ordered us to line up in a row, sit down on the ground and lay everything we were carrying in front of us. Juergen and I sat at the beginning of the line. The soldiers began to look through our knapsacks and the bags of the people near us and took what they wanted. We lost some of our food and a few little things, maybe a pen or pencil, I can't remember what it was. But there were no valuables to be had and they passed on down the line, shining their flashlights on the belongings of the other people.

Since the lineup was quite long they kept on walking farther away from us. Juergen whispered to me: "This is the time, let's run." And before I could even think about it he had grabbed my hand and dragged me into the darkness of the forest. A few yards away we crouched behind a bush and looked back.

When nobody seemed to have noticed that we were gone and the people who had sat near us did not indicate our absence either, we crawled on our hands and knees slowly and quietly, farther and farther away from the group in the direction that we thought would be west. My heart pounded like a steam engine and every two minutes or so Juergen stopped to listen if someone was following us. The voices became more distant and now we could be sure that the soldiers had not noticed our escape.

Eventually we got up and started to run, but because it was so dark we could not see where we were going. At one time we stumbled into a hole with blackberry bushes. I remember being entangled in the thorny branches that scratched my face and hands and ripped my clothes. I started to cry and wanted to give up, but Juergen scolded me, untangled me and pulled me forward. He was not going to give up after having made it this far!

Very carefully we now kept on walking westward, listening for footsteps other than ours and hoping that there were neither land mines nor electric wires. After a short while, maybe half an hour after our escape, we found ourselves at the edge of the forest. In front of us lay a very large freshly-plowed field and in the distance on the horizon we could see many lights, which we knew instinctively was Helmstedt, and safety. It seemed so very close, but there was this open field we had to cross and we did not know where the exact border line was.

We stood among the trees for the longest time watching and listening. When we were quite certain that no one seemed to be nearby, we dropped on our stomachs and crawled on our arms and knees along a furrow of this field, watching for possible wire fences. It seemed to me that we had crawled for hours, which of course it wasn't. The fear of either being shot, blown up by a mine or being electrocuted still had a strong grip on me and I was physically and emotionally so exhausted that I thought I just could not make it. Juergen kept on encouraging me, pushing and pulling me and telling me not to give up. I am eternally grateful to him for having gotten me across that fiendish border; without him I would have never been able to survive the ordeal.

We must have crawled for about half a mile like this, stopping from time to time for a short rest when we suddenly saw the silhouettes of two men coming towards us. We froze on the spot but as they came closer we heard them talk in German to each other. From what we could figure, one of them was a *Grenzgaenger* who took the other one across the border for a fee. We finally did sit up and asked them where we were. They confirmed that the lights in the distance indeed were the lights of Helmstedt and that we already had been on the western side for the last 200 meters or so. They were very interested where we had come from and wanted to know whether we had encountered border guards. We told them what we knew and then parted ways, from now on walking upright with a feeling of euphoria. We felt like singing and dancing, and did not care how dirty we were and how much difficulty we had just left behind us. We were free and safe! For no money in the world would I have wanted to switch places with the two men who were going to where we had just come from. Juergen and I sang and walked on clouds all the way to Helmstedt, which took us about another two hours before we got there. Those two hours were definitely the two most elated hours of my life so far.

Freedom at Last

WE ARRIVED IN HELMSTEDT shortly after midnight. There were still a lot of people up and about, mostly, it seemed, refugees from somewhere. We asked our way to the Red Cross mission and found it near the railroad station. We were lucky to hear that one upper bunk bed was left and after cleaning ourselves up a little we climbed in that bunk and slept on the straw mattress as though we were in paradise.

The first thing we did the next morning was to write a letter to our mother telling her that we finally had arrived and that she did not need to worry any more. We then explored the city and tried to find my friend Gerda. We discovered that the refugee camp in which she worked was in Marienthal, which was about eight kilometres northeast of Helmstedt, at the border. A short bus ride took us there. Gerda was happy to see me, showed us around and introduced us to some of the doctors and other nurses. I was assured that there would be some work for me. The first few nights I stayed with Gerda and her mother in Helmstedt where they lived in a little flat. Juergen only stayed one more night and then left, as he had planned to do all along, for the Rhine River, where he wanted to get hired onto a cargo ship, moving goods up and down the Rhine.

In 1934 with my favourite chicken, my younger brother Juergen (left), and Peter, a summer visitor to the village.

At four years old; Juregen is one. Note the clown face on the front of the cart.

Hille (right) and I play dress-up like the adult women.

Behind our garden, minding the geese. I started my love for needlework early.

Below: In the haystack, Herbert Butz, one of the summer guests we took in. He felt compelled to look under the bed each night, making sure there were no monsters lurking there. Seated at left, Wolfgang Mueller, Erika's younger brother, at 11. He died a year later.

1934, beside our apple trees. My mother sewed the dress for me— pink, with two flowers.

Left: Juergen's 4th birthday, 1932. Above, my dolls.

A day at Heidberg tower, age 14. Juergen is behind me, right, with his friend Paul.

Frieda, 1930. Juergen is two. Below, Juergen and me at 7 and 10.

A family photo, and a rare picture of my father. We always had a pile of sand in our backyard for play in the summer of 1939, before the war.

The main road through Brietzig as it appeared until 1945. Even in those days, this style of house, with the barns attached in the back, were protected as historic buildings. As of 1981, only one remained.

Our house in Brietzig from the rear. The outhouse was to the right. Photo taken ca. 1975.

Far left: picking grapes from the side of our house with Fritz, Hille's brother. He had been hired for the job, but I wanted to do it.

Left: sitting in one of our apple trees.

Below, the large tile stove, similar to what was in one of the bedrooms, which served to heat the upper floor.

The original mill, which burned down in 1936.

Brietzig pubic school and church tower, ca. 1968. The school had two classes, one from Grades 1 to 4, the other 5 through 8. Inset: the back of the school as it appeared in 1982. It has not changed very much. The sloped cover was removed to shovel coal into the cellar.

Period dress.

Unlike the school, the original mill has been almost completely destroyed. Left, as it appeared until 1945. Below, ca. 1982, closed and dilapidated.

January 1941, at Betty Bartel's (pictured centre) Dance Studio. This was the final gala ball. I'm seated bottom row, far left, with pig tails.

Right and below: Our first house party in summer of 1942 in our backyard, before the boys were drafted into the army. Only three would come back. The other three came to visit me many years later when I lived in Hespler.

Our second house party in the winter of 1943, which was encouraged by my mother. Everyone loved her, and we partied all night.

The next morning, of course, we all went to school, pictured here on our way to the train. These photos were taken by my mother.

Below, a professional photo taken at end of exams, March 17, 1943, with the only two boys remaining in our class. They were too young to be drafted at that time, however, they soon followed their friends into the army.

Left, my first boyfriend, Dieter Fewson (left) in 1940. He boarded with his friend, Peter Schulz. Peter was the son of our Burgermeister. His mother, his sister and my mother were the only ones to get out of Brietzig. Photo taken against the corrugated tin wall of "the hut", our train station.

An Abitur photo of the graduating high school girls, with the school director and our home room teacher.

My mother with one of our summer visitors from the city.

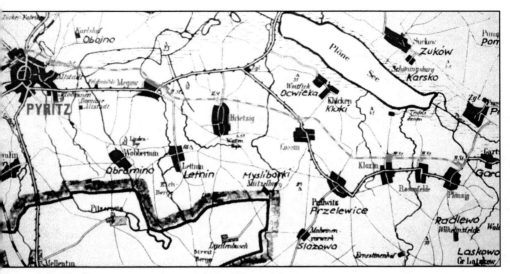

The route followed by our narrow-gauge train, so central to life in the village both before and during the war.

View from the Wartberg ("waiting mount") in Brietzig, looking down on the road taken by Bishop Otto von Bamberg on his way to Pyritz bringing baptism and Christianity. This same road was followed centuries later by the Russians, as they moved into our village from the East.

The labour camp in Tenzerow, where I started my "RAD dienst." There were 80 young girls housed in the facility, with six leaders.

Photo taken at Tenzerow on a Sunday afternoon; we are wearing the official uniform, but without hat and jacket. These were most of the 24 girls that were in my room.

Tenzerow: An instruction in arts and crafts.

Tenzerow. Annemie, who came to visit me in Canada, is second from left.

Dancing on a Sunday afternoon qualified as recreation at Tenzerow. In the foreground are two house leaders.

Below I am wearing my "working uniform" at Tenzerow: a red kerchief, white blouse, blue smock and red apron. A supervisor must have taken this picture. At right is the "official" photograph.

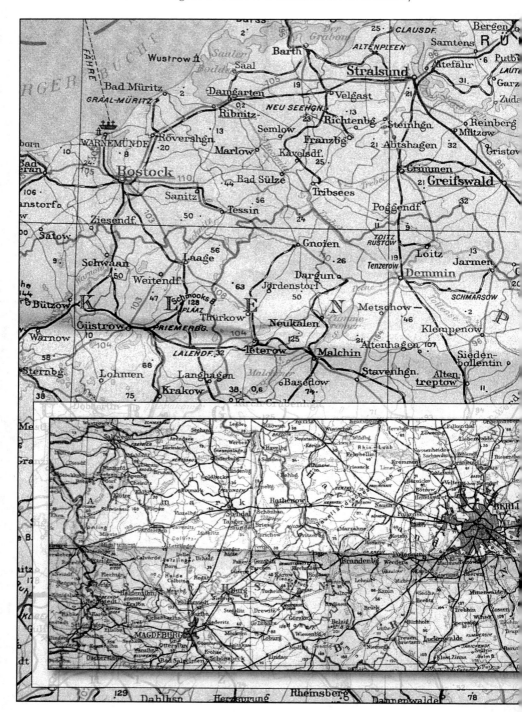

Dargun is as far as we made it on our initial trek out of Thurow. Inset: Juergen and I made our way by train, not to Rostock, but south to Berlin and then Magdeburg, on our way to the Black Border, and freedom.

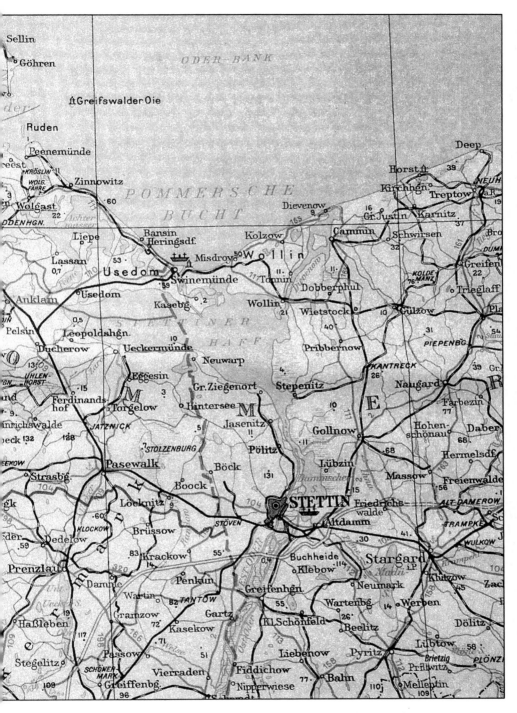

Ferdinandshof is where my mother and I were forced to turn around by the Mongols, as we attempted to return to our home in Brietzig.

Stone barracks at the munitions factory in Barth.

Above, "Adolf Hitler Strasse", in Lissa, as it was called at the time. My father's shop was the second on the left.

School's out, 1943: As the only two RAD "maiden" who had Grade 13, we were assigned to a school as teachers in Triebsees.

Wooden barracks at the RAD in Triebsees.

Entrance to the ballroom of the manor house in Thurow, 1944.

Ernst Krose and niece, December 1944.

The manor house, above, and Thurow in 1990 were in a sad state of repair. At right is the building from which I jumped to hide from the Russians in the rain barrel.

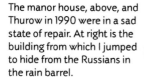

"Cow Corner": This is the barn in the school house yard, into which I lured the cow as it passed down the road. As it turned out, the cow was pregnant, and soon we had milk, and a calf to trade.

The old Thurow school house building, pictured here in 1990. The three of us lived in the upper room with the attic window. This was the window from which Juergen lowered me down with the improvised bed sheet rope to escape from the Russians, again.

Post war: I am accepted as a Red Cross nurse in 1946-47 in Mariental.

Instructing a class in traffic safety. The sign behind me urges, "Eyes open!"

The WP, "Weibliche Polizei", a new organization that admitted women into the police force for the first time. I am third from left.

Heinz in uniform, going off to work as a police driver.

I become a plain clothes detective.

The dance in Helmsteadt that Heinz could not attend, before we were married. He gave permission only when my mother agreed to come along as a chaperone. Juergen came too.

Heinz's mother and father are seated front row left, with Theo, Heinz's brother. The flower girl is my cousin Utta. Juergen stands behind my mother with Heinz's sister Mathilde, right, with whom he had recently broken a romantic relationship, much to her dismay and that of her mother.

I marry Heinz, September 9, 1950. Below, with my mother.

An early family photo with Gert in Salzgitter. Gert was the centre of our universe at a very early age. Heinz bought the most beautiful, most expensive carriage he could find on the day the baby was born.

Left, 69 Breite Str. My mother and Juergen are at the window. I am crouched with Gert below.

Juergen leaves Salzgitter by train, bound for Canada. A year later, we join him. The day after we arrived in Troy, at Sagers. Juergen's fiancée, Anne, came to visit. Mrs. Sager was a very generous and friendly host. Mr. Sager seems almost hidden in the background.

Above, our first billet in Canada: the Sager farmhouse near Troy, Ontario.

Downtown Tavistock, Ontario, in the 1950s.

Pastor Stockman.

Berlin, December 1957. My mother leaves for Canada, surrounded by relatives and friends.

Still wearing the same outfit, my mother arrives.

Juergen's and Anne's house on Willard Gardens, Toronto. Roland wears a sweater with his telephone number on it, in case he ever got lost. No one would think of doing something like that in these days.

Clarkson, Ontario.

Happy times in High Park.

Pioneers at the cottage.

Our first house on Zorra Street—cleared long ago to make way for condos. Below, our first car: a green, 1949 Mercury.

The party's at my house: Heinz and I with our good friends, Frank and Muriel.

My first teaching job in Canada, and my first class.

Holy Angels Catholic School.

...and my final staff the year I retired in 1990, at James Culnan School.

Sunnyside Park, on Lake Ontario
in Toronto.

A Sunday walk with the two crown princes, 1956.

CHAPTER NINE

Life on the Other Side

A few days later I was given a striped uniform and officially became a Red Cross nurse. I remember that early on, Gerda shared a chocolate bar with me. I had not seen chocolate for years. It seemed to me that I had arrived in the land of milk and honey. I ate half of it and wrapped the other small piece in some wax paper and sent it to Thurow to my mother.

My duty, together with that of about a dozen other young girls, was to receive the sick refugees who arrived daily at the nearby station in the Red Cross freight car, one of those that Juergen and I had planned to hop into in Magdeburg. Marienthal was an old army camp with mainly wooden barracks, several big hangars and a large latrine barrack in the middle that consisted of one room only. It featured about a dozen wooden seats on each side without any partitions whatsoever. One of the hangars housed an enormous kitchen where daily meals were cooked for thousands of people. The other buildings, even bigger and with straw covered floors, were used as sleeping quarters for the many refugees that arrived every day and usually stayed one night before being transported further inland. Other barracks served as eating rooms, registration and disinfection rooms.

Each person arriving had to undergo a procedure where they were sprayed from head to toe, even under their clothes, with DDT powder, a poison that was banned many years later. It effectively killed any lice or other bugs. Today I wonder what effect that powder might have had on the people whose job it was, day after day, to spray the new arrivals with this poison.[1] Sometimes up to 1,500 refugees would arrive on one train, and frequently more than one train per day had to be processed.

One barrack was designated as sick bay. Four or five doctors and several trained nurses looked after the seriously ill people. Many of the workers in the camp were refugees themselves, so several barracks had been furnished with some essentials and served as living quarters for the workers. I, too, was assigned a bed in one of the rooms that I shared with three other young girls who had been hired as "nurses". It reminded me very much of my time in the *Arbeitsdienst*, the work camp which I had had to attend a few years earlier. The skills that we all had learned in these camps came in handy now. We developed a beautiful comradeship, shared, helped and consoled each other when the worries for our lost families became too overpowering. We became each other's family.

We saw a lot of human suffering in this camp among the arrivals. One old woman we had just unloaded died right there at the station in my lap. Many others died a few hours after their arrival, mostly old people who just gave up. It wasn't too bad during the summer when the nights were warm. But some trains took three or four days before they arrived in our camp, and often we removed frozen bodies from the train during the winter of 1946-47. It was especially sad when the bodies were those of small children. Other children came in with third degree frozen hands, feet and ears and had to undergo amputations. It was terrible to see the suffering and not being able to help. By this time we all had received some training in nursing and were able to help out and assist the doctors with minor cases.

I had worked and lived in this camp for several months, it was still warm weather in 1946, when one day Juergen suddenly reappeared.

---

1   I remember that both my mother and I had once contracted head lice in Thurow after the war. Heaven knows where we picked them up. We both covered our heads and hair for a few days with DDT, which I found in a storage barn, and the lice disappeared.

He had tried the life on the riverboats but his knee injury caused him constant pain in the dampness of that climate and he had to give it up. Since I was his only known contact in West Germany, he came back to Helmstedt with the intention of finding work there. Of course, we were both happy to see each other again and because of the volume of arriving refugees there was great need for workers in our camp. Juergen was hired immediately to work in the registration office. Unfortunately, all the living quarters in the camp were filled and he had to find himself a room in the nearby village of Grasleben.

We had been in constant contact with our mother by mail and knew that she was trying to join us, but she did not quite seem to know how to go about it. We had told her to try the Red Cross car in Magdeburg again. Whatever we had owned in Thurow was not worth worrying over, she should just leave everything behind and come, as we had done, with a knapsack. Because of our horrendous experience crossing into the west we did not dare to go back to get her.

One afternoon in late summer of 1946 after we had waited routinely for the next train to arrive, I began to help unload the sick people from the Red Cross car, and whom should I find among them? *Our mother!*

We both couldn't believe it. We cried and laughed, and again I had this overwhelming feeling of gratitude that I had experienced when I first knew we were safe on that open field. Because of my mother's bad health and her constant asthma, I had been very worried about her and wasn't really all that sure whether she would ever be able to make it.[2] She had followed our suggestions, had taken the train to Magdeburg, had been able to reach the Red Cross car without being seen by the guards and had found a sympathetic nurse in the car who had pulled her in. The nurse bandaged her face and arms up and put her in one corner. When the train stopped at the Russian control point where we had been driven out of the train, she and the other ill people were left in peace, nobody counted heads and she was free. Again she had brought the gold watch

---

2   Unlike Juergen and me, my mother did not need a permit to use the train because she was "too old" and not healthy enough to work, so nobody cared what she did. They were glad to get rid of her. She just took a bag and left, with the watch in a syrup jar.

from my father with her in a sugar beet syrup jar, the only valuable thing we ever kept of all our belongings in Brietzig.

My brother and I asked the camp manager for a job for our mother in the registration office and she began working there the following day. She moved in with Juergen in Grasleben where the two shared a room. They had to walk to work each day about two kilometres, but we all ate at the camp free and earned enough money to pay the rent. We could easily have afforded a larger place but there was just no flat to be had anywhere, not even two rooms.

The camp existed until the following spring, April or May 1947, when all refugees had been driven out of the former German provinces of Pommerania and Selesia, and the trains stopped coming. This meant unemployment for a very large group of people, including the three of us.

Goldsmith and Police Officer

I FOUND A VERY SMALL ROOM in Helmstedt which I rented from a couple. It was wide enough for a bed and a chair and long enough for the bed and a wardrobe in which the woman kept her clothes. Our mother and Juergen stayed in Grasleben. We now had to find some other means to support ourselves.

My mother started to give some piano lessons to children of local families who had not suffered any material losses. My brother began working in a former large salt mine in Grasleben that had been stocked during the war with live ammunition. Now all this ammunition had to be brought out again. It was an extremely dangerous job. My mother worried every day whether she would see my brother again in the evening, but the pay was good and there was no other work available in the village. On the other hand, there were jobs in Helmstedt, but no rooms for rent. One day I saw a sign in the window of the local goldsmith store: "Apprentice Wanted". I remembered that my RAD friend, Annemie Eckhardt, was a goldsmith, so I decided I might try this as well. My enthusiasm did not last very long.

The owner was an arrogant, bossy and unfriendly bachelor who just seemed to need someone to wash the floors of the premises. He already had two male helpers and made no attempt to show me any of the skills I wanted to learn. When I requested that he do so, he once let me melt some metal and in the evenings I was allowed to put the tools away. He even requested me to come in on Saturdays and Sundays to clean the store and the work rooms. The weekly pay was 12 Marks, of which I had to pay 8 for rent. I had no opportunity to cook or even to heat a cup of milk. If I wanted something warm to eat I had to go to the community kitchen, which was the place where the homeless could buy a cup of soup for 25 pennies. I did this quite often but they served mainly pea and bean soup, and I am convinced this is where I began to develop the gall bladder stones which later caused a dangerous operation, which I almost did not survive.

I still loved to dance and saw an ad that announced tap dancing lessons. I ate even less and with the rest of the money enrolled myself in a tap class. However, after about four weeks I became so weak that even with great effort I could not bring up the energy anymore to continue the dancing.

One day in a bakery I met a young woman in police uniform. We began to talk and had a cup of coffee together in the local coffee shop. During the conversation, I told her of my sorry situation while she told me that she was an officer in the newly-established female police department. She also mentioned that there was just now an ad in the paper for the hiring of some more young women.

My interest perked up right away. I bought a paper and the same day sent a letter off with the request for an application. In my earlier years I had a few times contemplated joining the police. I had always been adventurous and excited about the unusual. A few days thereafter, I received a letter asking me for an interview in Braunschweig. I remember I took a bus there, on Thursday, August 21. It was 1947. I had told Mr. Moelders, the goldsmith, that I was not coming in that day and did not care that he got angry. At the Police Office in Braunschweig they asked me about my education and what I had done in the past. They let me write a short dictation and gave me some simple math questions and accepted me on the spot. The only hindrance had been that I was too young. They only wanted women 23 years of age or older. However, since I had done well on the tests and was only a few months away from my 23rd birthday they made an exception. It gave me tremendous pleasure to go back the next day to the goldsmith to tell him that, as of today, I was quitting.

A few days after this happened I was sent to the police academy in Hannoversch-Muenden for the period of four months. The area there is very beautiful, and I have these four months in fondest memory for several reasons.

Most of all I liked to learn. Each day we had classes in different subjects, all police or law related and I soaked up everything trying to be one of the top students in the class. There were eight young women including myself, and a few hundred young men being trained at this academy. Aside from the academic lessons we had physical exercises, learned how to march and how to shoot and, of course, the eight of us had plenty of opportunities to meet young men.

There I met Oswald Stastny, with whom I really fell in love, and Werner Tiefenbach, who fell in love with me. We would all go out on our free evenings in groups to the local coffee shops where we ordered the so-called *Heissgetraenk*, some kind of hot, coloured sugar water that tasted better than champagne to us. We often took long walks where the rivers Fulda and Werra meet, but I was never alone with Oswald. Werner, on the other hand, managed quite often to follow me when he saw that I was alone, and spared no words telling me how smitten he was with me. At the time I was flattered, but not interested. After we all had passed our final exams we were assigned to different police departments.

Oswald was sent to the police force in Hannover. I served the first two weeks in Watenstedt and was then transferred to Helmstedt, where Werner already had been stationed. He and I eventually became engaged, since Oswald obviously did not return my feelings for him. At least, I thought Werner and I were engaged. He had told me that he was going to marry me, and I had said yes. He did not give me a ring but that did not really bother me because we did not earn much money. In my innocence and stupidity, I believed him and it took quite some time before I found out that he had told the same thing to other girls too.

I know that my mother did not like him very much. I had met his mother once and she had warned me, saying that I should not keep my hopes up, he was not the marrying kind. Of course, I did not believe her but he betrayed me more than once.

We did the usual things, went for bike rides, played table tennis and went dancing. Once he told me that he had invited an old friend to Helmstedt for the upcoming police ball and I should be understanding to let him see her that one last time. I was understanding and at the evening of the ball, he sat with this woman I did not know and danced with her while I sat with a group of other policemen and their wives and friends at a different table.

Eventually I became impatient and went myself to ask him for a dance. He was not very pleased about it and found a few excuses why he had to be alone with that woman. I was miffed for several days but since she had left Helmstedt again the following day I eventually forgave him, until...

Several weeks later he came to ask me for a favour. He said he had contracted Malaria during the war as a soldier and since I knew this particular doctor very well from my work at the refugee camp, he would like me to go to him and ask him for quinine. I told him to get it himself. Again he found some excuse which I don't remember, but which at the time seemed to make sense to me. I went to the doctor and he asked me whether I was pregnant. I barely knew what that meant, let alone what connection my request had to do with something like that. I told the doctor why I had asked for it. Needless to say, I did not get the quinine.

Later I told the whole story to another, older police woman on the force with whom I was very friendly. She was aghast at the audacity of Tiefenbach to put such a request to me, and explained that he likely needed the quinine for an abortion for another girlfriend of his. Needless to say, the phony engagement was off immediately and I was really very glad to have gotten rid of him.

Not long after this episode, a young officer came to Helmstedt who was two years younger than I was. Very soon we started a friendship, and got along very well together. He was tall, blond, very kind, educated and had excellent manners. He really was everything that I liked in a man. After about six or eight months, he actually asked me to marry him. I was flabbergasted because I had never thought of a serious relationship with him because he simply was "too young". Tradition had taught me that a man had to be older, so this was out of the question.

Besides myself, there was just one other woman on the police force in Helmstedt. We had become friends and often I stayed the night with her in her parents' house. In the meantime I had managed to find another accommodation in Helmstedt—a very large room in a house that belonged to an elderly lady. I took my mother in with me, since her room in Grasleben was not much better than the one we had had in Thurow. So I actually had two places where I could stay, though neither of them was a real home.

Juergen had by now also quit his job in the mine and had joined the police force. At the beginning of 1948 he attended the same academy from which I had previously graduated.

Since Helmstedt was a border town, a lot of smuggling went on between East and West Germany. One of the duties of our police force was to catch these smugglers who dealt in all things imaginable, from fish oil to clothes, to light-weight furniture. Silk stockings were a valuable commodity. Once or twice weekly, we held raids, usually during the night, and confiscated the contraband. Whoever ended up with it and what was done with it I often wondered but never found out. I always had the sneaking suspicion that some of it ended up in the apartment of our "inspector", the official title of the head of our organization. He was a very short man around 45 years old with a big mouth who bellowed orders and bullied most of the men. We called him the "little Napoleon". Toward my female colleague and myself, his manners were a bit more restrained.

One specific duty the two of us had was to visit the local schools and the schools in neighbouring villages, to teach traffic rules and give general safety lessons. I enjoyed this interaction with the children and teachers, and tried to make it as interesting for them as possible by taking them out on the road and assigning them roles to play.

After several months, my colleague, Ilse Schaper, and I were assigned to the plainclothes detective department: the *Kripo*, short for *Kriminalpolizei*. From now on we wore civilian clothes and had to work with criminal cases, mainly with women, teenagers and children. We now had a new boss and were trained on the job on how to investigate cases, how to write down complaints and reports, and how to interrogate a suspect as well as question witnesses. I became involved in murder cases, kidnappings, child molestations, rape cases, abortions and thefts of all kinds and learned a lot about what makes people tick, good and bad. I remember looking once for a newborn baby that had disappeared, and finding it wrapped in a bag in some kind of swamp.

Another time I was involved in a murder-suicide case. A four year old child drowned while the mother swam to shore again. She had intended to drown herself and her daughter. Often I had to accompany female prisoners to court or to the prison in Braunschweig.

Still another case very vivid in my memory is one of a murderer who had escaped from prison and had been sighted in Helmstedt. We had an informer working for us who told us to look for him in a stretch of forest outside the city. A group of us surrounded that forest during the night, long before the sun came up. I was sent into the forest as "bait", with two policemen close behind me. We followed a narrow pathway and after several hundred feet I saw the man lying in the grass, sleeping. I remember that beside him lay a dead goose that probably was to have been his next meal. My two colleagues pounced on him and put him into handcuffs. There were many times when, in retrospect, I did not realize how dangerous the situation was for me. This was a case in point, and at this and some other events, I wore a pistol. Most days I did not. The excitement always gave me a thrill and I felt rather important being part of a group that tried to bring back law and order to the country. I enjoyed what I was doing and looked at each day as being a new adventure.

Frequently we raided movie theatres, checking the passports of the people in the theatre and pulling out everyone under the age of 21 if the movie was a restricted one. Times certainly have changed since then.

In the winter of 1948, I contracted pneumonia and pleurisy and became extremely ill. My doctor was the same one whom I had met in the refugee camp and whom I had asked for the quinine. He still had connections to the English troops and managed to get penicillin for me. He told me that I was the first German person in the hospital who had ever been treated with this medication. I remained in the hospital for two months, the first few weeks hanging on by a thread. It was obviously not yet my time to leave this plane.

In March, I was sent for four weeks to a recuperation home for police staff in Braunlage in the Harz mountains. Those four weeks were the happiest and most carefree days I had had for years and I cherish the memory of the beautiful scenery and the wonderful comradeship that I developed with those who had been sent there to recover their health. I remember daily health baths in whirlpools with pine scented water, massages with fragrant oils, open air concerts on Sunday afternoons and long walks through the mountains in the warm sun, with the snow still glistening on the ground.

Coming back to Helmstedt, I met a newly appointed police officer my own age with whom I started a friendship. His first name was Rudi—I forgot his last name. He had been born in the Ukraine to German parents. His father apparently had been a diplomat in Kiev. This, of course, reminded me again of my Russian POW friend, Ivan, whose home also had been Kiev, and who now lay dead somewhere in a forest near Rostock.

When the war started, Rudi's family had tried to hide out in Moskau with friends. But they were found and the parents had been taken away. Rudi did not know whether they were dead or had been transported into labour camps. Somehow he had managed as a young boy to get behind the German front line and had been shipped to Germany where he had been drafted during the last year of the war. We liked each other and did the usual things together, played table tennis, took walks and bike rides.

One day he told me that it would be better if we didn't see each other any longer in our spare time. I was quite sad about this and wanted to know the reason, but he did not give me an explanation and our friendship ended. Then, after I had been stationed in Helmstedt for about two years, I was transferred to Salzgitter-Lebenstedt in the fall of 1949. I had not been there very long when I heard that Rudi had committed suicide by throwing himself in front of a moving train. Apparently some Russian agents had pressured him to act as a spy in the police force and he did not know how to escape from them. I never discovered the details of the story, but here was yet another young promising life that the horrors of the war had claimed. This event depressed me for weeks and only then did I understand why he had not wanted me to see him any more. He was probably trying to protect me.

Lebenstedt was a dreary, monotonous city. It had been built during the war years and consists to this day only of concrete row houses that look like an army camp. I rented a room across from the office in a flat that belonged to a young widow and her mother. In Lebenstedt, I met a refugee from East Prussia, my new colleague, Marta Neumann, who became my friend for life. Often we worked on the same cases and spent much of our free time together. Lebenstedt had been a group of villages that had been amalgamated into the city of Salzgitter. Juergen had been transferred at about the same time to Salzgitter-Bad, the largest and oldest of the community groups, about 20 kilometres south of Salzgitter-Lebenstedt, and a much prettier, long established town.

Because of the distances that had to be covered between the villages that now made up the "city", and although we all had bicycles, more often than not we needed a car to get from A to B. Most of us did not drive and there were designated drivers that had to be ready for us to get to the crime location or to court. Cars were still a novelty in the country, but having had the privilege as a child to ride in my father's car, I now, after so many years, enjoyed these car rides especially. Quite often it was also a police bus in which we were driven, for example, if a woman or a teenager had to be transported to jail or court, I was usually the one who had to accompany them in one of our vehicles. A few times, I remember also riding in the sidecar of a motorbike.

Sometime in 1949, after several months and considerable negotiations, Juergen and I found a little flat in Salzgitter-Bad at the outskirts of town in one of the newer war-time buildings that looked much like the houses in Lebenstedt. It was on the second floor, Breite Str. 69. Again, after much bureaucracy, writing letters to city hall and the housing commission, we finally managed to receive permission to let our mother come from Helmstedt to live with us in Salzgitter-Bad.

For several months I kept my room in Lebenstedt for convenience, and also because the flat was too small for four people. It belonged to a divorced man who needed some income, and who had agreed to let Juergen and my mother live in his flat. It consisted of one bedroom, which he kept for himself, a very tiny living room which was about eight feet square, a kitchen and a bathroom with a toilet and a sink. It had neither a bathtub nor a shower. Juergen slept in the kitchen on a bed with an iron frame, our mother slept in the living room on a tiny sofa and the owner of the flat lived in the "large" bedroom. The kitchen had a coal stove that was supposed to heat the whole flat. In the winter it was freezing cold. Every morning the fire had to be stoked, but coal was hard to come by and we often went into nearby forests to gather branches to burn. Eventually Juergen organized a small electric heater for the living room. We were very lucky because the man from whom we sublet moved out after several months and at that time, I also moved to Salzgitter-Bad into the flat with my mother and Juergen.

Now we lived in luxury, because we actually had a bedroom, which my mother and I shared while Juergen had a cot in the kitchen. I took a public bus every morning to work in Lebenstedt, but a short while later was transferred to Salzgitter-Bad.

Heinz

IN LEBENSTEDT I MET MY FUTURE husband, Heinz, who was a uniformed police officer and who worked as one of the designated drivers. He was a good-looking young man, handsome in the uniform (I always worked in plainclothes), had a friendly smile and walked with an energetic stride. I liked him.

At the end of the year, a dance was arranged for everyone connected to the police force. Since I absolutely loved to dance, I had long looked forward to this evening. As it turned out, Heinz asked me to dance with him almost every single dance. He wanted me to promise him not to dance with anyone else that night, which I could not do. But he kept on staying close by and before anyone else had a chance to ask me, he was already there. The few times he missed, he became quite jealous and angry at the other men who danced with me. I should have heard some warning bells ringing, but instead I thought it to be quite flattering and I did not mind at all, mainly because he was an excellent dancer. Years later this jealousy destroyed our marriage.

Heinz was Catholic and I was Lutheran. At the beginning of March 1950, Heinz asked me to marry him. He wanted me to become Catholic. I was not fanatical about religion; I believed in God and in a world beyond our visible dimensions. I did not think that God cared whether one was Catholic or Lutheran or whatever. The question of religion was not a big stumbling block for me.

My mother, on the other hand, did not like the idea at all. She was rather upset and let me know that she did not think that this was the right man for me. However, since I was 25 and she had already talked me out of one marriage, she did not want to interfere and let me make my own decision. I can imagine that I most likely stated stubbornly that I was old enough to know what I wanted.

Aside from the fact that Heinz was good looking and very attentive, I thought that I was most likely going to have very good-looking children if I married him. I also believed that I was very old already, and soon nobody would want me anymore. I had just gotten over the unrequited love for Oswald and still felt somewhat rejected and unworthy. And also, I had said "yes" when Heinz had first asked me, so how could I back out now? A promise is a promise is a promise, and keeping it is the honourable thing to do.

We got engaged on March 9, 1950, exactly six months after we had talked to each other for the first time. During our engagement over the next six months, several incidents happened that made me aware of the extreme jealousy Heinz exhibited.

I especially remember two other dances that took place during this time. One we attended together in Salsgitter. During the evening a few of our colleagues asked me to dance. Heinz did not like this at all and made sure that he always was the first one to ask me. Then, while Heinz was probably at the bar, another policeman who happened to be married asked me for a dance. Heinz threw a tantrum. He made such a terrible scene with that man that it ended up in a regular fight. He then took me outside and yelled at me in a reproachful voice as though I had just openly committed an act of prostitution. He turned and left me standing there crying uncontrollably. I was so devastated that I thought I could not go on living, knowing that I had to marry this man. The only solution I could see at that moment was to throw myself in front of a car.

At that time not many people had cars. I must have stood there for at least 20 minutes and only three cars had gone by. Each time I started into the road, I got frightened at the last second and stopped. I thought Heinz would come back out and look for me, but he probably was too busy accusing the other policeman of "trying to break up our engagement." I do not remember how I got home that evening. The following day Heinz was very apologetic and I forgave him because I let him convince me that he had done it for my own protection.

The next dance took place in Helmstedt, which meant that I had to take the train and stay overnight at my friend's house if I wanted to attend. Since I knew everyone on the force there and loved to dance I was very eager to go. He could not come along because he had to work that night. After several days of lengthy arguments, tears on my part and stony silences on his part, I finally got his "permission" to go if my mother would come along as a chaperone. At the last minute my brother also got the day off and the three of us went without Heinz. We had a great time and I danced to my heart's content. On my return I had to report in detail how often and with whom I had danced and talked during the evening. I did not tell him how much I had enjoyed the evening without him, but I wished I was not engaged to him anymore. However, I was, and such a commitment you just did not break. What would all our colleagues say? Besides, once we were married, he would change because then there would be no more reason for him to be jealous; or so I thought.

On September 9, 1950, we were married. I remember a comment he made a week before this day. He said to me: "Only seven more days, I can hardly wait." In response my thoughts were: "I wished it were another 70 years." But now there was no going back anymore and I always tried to "behave" the way he wanted me to.

For instance, I wasn't allowed to wear lipstick. One time I did and he made me take it off at once and told me to never, ever do that again, or else. What that "else" was, I don't know, but I was afraid enough of him and did not do it anymore. I always tried to avoid talking to men, colleagues or otherwise, when he was around. When we were alone, he was attentive, kind and considerate to me and could at times be very funny, but as soon as others were around I knew I had to be on my guard if I did not want to cause a scene.

My friend, Marta, was also eventually transferred to Salzgitter-Bad. Even of her, Heinz became terribly jealous when I made a date with her for a visit in the evening, or on a weekend afternoon. She never visited me because Heinz did not leave us alone, and often made caustic remarks about her, so I had to neglect my friendship with her just to stop Heinz from being angry at me all the time. Unfortunately this behaviour, which I abided for many years, caused me to lose my own identity and I often felt like a mouse in a trap.

Our wedding day, however, was a happy occasion. He picked me up in the morning at 8:30 at Breite Str. 69. We walked to the City Hall for the civil ceremony. The church wedding was scheduled for noon, which gave me enough time to change into my wedding dress that a seamstress had sewn for me.

The church was about two kilometres from our flat, which we figured was too far for everyone to walk. So we had rented a bus that picked up the guests at Heinz's parents' house first, and then came to my mother's flat to pick us up. For the previous two or three months I had taken Catholic instruction in private lessons, and was now considered to be ready. I had learned all the correct responses by heart but the doctrine had no logic to me and I did not understand Catholicism any better than I had before the lessons.

The priest rejoiced of my soul having been saved by my true belief. He baptized and confirmed me before the wedding ceremony. Of the ceremony itself I have no recollection, not even of the "I do". I was just extremely tense and only knew that this was a definite end and a definite beginning. The reception was held in the house of Heinz's parents, who had emptied one room on the second floor for us, which from then on was to be our home. There were about 20 people at the wedding, neighbours mainly. From my side were my mother, my brother and an 11 year old cousin, Uta Kerbs, the daughter of my mother's younger sister, who had carried my veil. Since there was a lot to eat, the guests came back for the next two days and everybody had a great time. Heinz and I had one week of holidays, but since we did not have enough money there was no honeymoon trip to anywhere.

Heinz now worked in Salzgitter-Bad permanently, as did Juergen. The two of them were in the uniformed force, while I worked for the *Kriminalpolizei* as a plainclothes detective. We worked out of two different offices, which was a blessing for me, because I had to deal all the time with male colleagues. With Heinz in the same office all sorts of unfortunate situations could have developed.

For the first few months things went fine. We both had jobs and a fairly good income. I had two homes to go to: the one room in his parent's house and my mother's flat, where I was more often than not. I thought the fits of jealousy might be over by now. But in December he accused me of being unfaithful because I had attended a staff Christmas party at my office. It was such a horrible scene that I felt I just had to make an end of it. I remember that that winter was very cold and snowy. After he had left, I put on a summer dress and ran out into the forest behind the house where I trudged through the snow for more than an hour, determined to get a lung infection and die from it. When that did not happen, I bought bitter almonds, soaked them in water for a day and then tried to drink the suds. But the taste was so awful it made me vomit. I then decided that I probably was meant to live and that dying would be an easy way out. In no way did I want to be considered a coward.

I began reading every psychology book I could get my hands on and tried to learn to understand the actions of a jealous person. It occurred to me that Heinz might have felt abandoned as a child of 13, when his parents moved from Kamp-Lintford in the west of the country to Salzgitter, taking his sister with them, but leaving him behind with some relatives. Another factor may have been his being drafted into the navy when he was 17, having served on a U-boat and having been bombed for days while underwater. Though he had been fished out of the ocean by the attacking American destroyer, he again had been left alone and was thrown into a POW camp in Arizona, in a strange country, with a strange language.

I remember discussing my troubled marriage and relationship with our police psychologist at the office and at a visit in her home. But she was not of much help. As far as her advice went, she felt I had to figure this out for myself. From then on I began to make excuses for him be-cause I saw a reason behind his often bizarre behaviour.

I also came to know his mother, since we lived in the same house, and realized that she was extremely bossy, moody and opinionated. I now had to weigh every word not just with my husband, but also with his mother. I could not please her. She always had something to com-plain about me. To Heinz she said: "What do you want with her, she is nothing and has nothing." Heinz's father, on the other hand, was a very kind and open-minded man. I liked him a lot and could talk to him about all sorts of topics, even about the sorry state of our marriage. He was very sad but urged me to stick it out with his son. They had another young son, Theo, who was five years old when we married, and was 23 years younger than Heinz. I liked him and he often came into our room and I would tell him all the fairy tales I knew from my childhood. Many years later he told me that he had never forgotten this, and that he had always loved me.

My brother, Juergen, had gone out with Heinz's sister, Mathilde, for awhile but after a few weeks the relationship soured and Juergen stopped seeing her. This change made Heinz's mother and Mathilde extremely angry at Juergen and, by association, at my mother and me, and the situation in the house became even more tense and cold. They refused to talk to my mother anymore, and were constantly making derogatory comments about her and my brother to Heinz and me. Eventually it became so unbearable that both of us avoided meeting the rest of his family at all, and any communication broke down.

We had been married for a year when we had some money saved and decided to go on a belated honeymoon. We had two weeks of holiday time coming but did not really know where to go. One day Heinz came home to tell me that he had arranged transportation for us to go to Bavaria. He had met a truck driver from the south who had delivered some goods to a store in Salzgitter and was scheduled to return the next day. Heinz had asked whether we could hitch a ride with him, and he had agreed. I quickly packed a suitcase and the following day we found ourselves in the back of a truck heading for Bavaria. It was a ride with many stops. The truck stopped in all sorts of small places, loading and unloading wares. We had come as far south as Fuerth near Nuernberg when we decided to take a train to Fuessen and from there to Neuschwanstein. There we found a Bed and Breakfast Inn and had a lovely holiday, visiting King Ludwig's castles and climbing the nearby mountains. For our return to Salzgitter, we took a train.

In June, 1952, our little Gert was born. I had stayed the last few days prior with my mother and Juergen at Breite Str. 69 and there, at 3:15 a.m., with the help of a midwife and with my mother and Heinz present, Gert decided to try out life on this plane. The birth was relatively easy, in as much as I had only been in labour for four hours. We were overjoyed and proud as punch. Heinz forgot the silent war with his parents and woke them up with the good news, then he went at 7 o'clock into town to buy the prettiest and most expensive baby carriage he could find. It was green and the sides were made of wicker. My mother and the midwife made me stay in bed for about two weeks which I could hardly stand, but that was how it was done at the time. After another week I went back to work. The police office was only about 10 minutes walking time away, so it was possible for me to go home several times during the day to nurse the baby, who stayed with my mother until the evenings when we took him back with us to our one-room home. This went on for about nine months.

The first year of Gert's life was probably the happiest in our marriage. We both were so occupied and happy with our little baby that we did not have time nor cared for other people, and lived just for ourselves. Since Heinz was happy all the time about having the two of us for himself and I did not miss the company of anyone else, we led a harmonious and quiet life.

CHAPTER TEN

Goodbye to Germany

E ven before I was married, Juergen and I had always wanted to leave
Germany and immigrate to somewhere far away from war and fighting. It did not really matter to us where we would end up. We had considered and made applications to Australia, South America, the U.S.A. and
Canada. For me, the main reason was that I did not feel safe in Germany
anymore. I had seen too many horrible things—what mankind could do
to each other, and I was afraid that Europe might become involved in
another war. Under no circumstances did I want my children to become
cannon fodder. Besides, I thought, it would be a lot easier to be killed by
a bomb than again having to face another human being aiming a pistol
or bayonet at me. Our mother agreed with us. She felt that there did not
seem to be much future for the two of us in Germany. I believe that she
too had had enough of fighting and wars. In the First World War she had
lost her first fiancé; the second war had taken her husband and almost
her son. She wanted us to live in safety.

A few weeks after Gert was born we received a letter informing us
that the Lutheran Church was sponsoring young people who wished to
immigrate to Canada and asked whether we were still interested. Juergen
saw his opportunity and applied. For me the situation had changed, even
though Heinz was willing for all of us to emigrate to Canada. We came
to the decision that Juergen should become the trailblazer and that we

would follow when Gert was a little older.

The requirement for a paid voyage by ship was that each applicant had to work for one year, either in a factory, on a farm or as a woodcutter in Canada, free of charge, in order to repay the debt to the church. Juergen was willing to do that, especially since he had befriended Anne Klatt, who also wished to immigrate to Canada to be with her sister, Lydia, who was married and lived in Toronto.

Juergen applied for farm work. By the spring of 1953, he had all the papers together, had passed all the health and political tests and one day in April of that year we saw him off at the little train station in Salzgitter, leaving for the "New World". Neither he nor we had any idea where fate would guide him. All we knew was that he travelled toward an uncertain future. It must have been very hard for my mother to let him go again, this time across the ocean! Only years later did I appreciate her courage when my own sons grew up and left me waving goodbye to them. It was then I remembered that April day, and gathered courage from the memory of my mother.

In the first letter we received from Juergen he told us what had happened to him after his arrival in Canada. Together with all the other young people, he had landed in Halifax and was transported west by train. He and many others were told to leave the train in a small town, called Kitchener, in the province of Ontario. They were guided into a huge hall where they were seated on benches along the walls. Shortly thereafter, a group of farmers entered who were all looking for farmhands. They looked over the young immigrants and asked each one to show their hands. Those who had calluses and looked like musclemen were picked up immediately. Juergen was apparently not so lucky, or, as it turned out, he was the lucky one. His hands were white and soft since he did not have to do any manual work in the police force, so he was passed by. At the end only he and one other boy were left. He told us that he had been very discouraged and felt humiliated. Finally, one farmer had pity on him and told him to come along with him.

His name was Lawrence Sager *(pronounced Sayger)* and he had a farm in Troy, near St. George and Brantford. Juergen wrote how kind and considerate both Mr. and Mrs. Sager were, and that he tried to show his gratitude by working extra hard on the farm and in the fields. After a few days he developed terrible blisters on his hands and had to wear gloves, but in time his hands toughened up. The Sagers were very appreciative of his efforts and as the year progressed they treated him more and more like their own son.

Each of Juergen's letters brought us new sensational reports. We heard that he and Mr. Sager would ride to the field in a car and that there was a radio in the cow barn because the cows liked music and gave more milk. He sent us some photographs of the huge house with three cars parked in front of it on a circular driveway. He told us about the delicious meals Mrs. Sager would cook, and described the interior of the house into whose living room our whole flat would easily have fit. We were just flabbergasted about all those strange things and the apparent affluence, and could hardly wait to read what wonders we would find out about in the next letter.

As soon as Juergen left Germany, I became more and more restless, and kept after Heinz to apply for our own immigration. Heinz was not at all opposed to emigrating to Canada or anywhere else for that matter. In Arizona he had learned to speak English quite well and was more fluent than I was with my half-forgotten school English. Besides that, he had run into some difficulties in the police force with his superiors and he was not happy with his work anymore. Maybe he also liked the idea of getting me away from all those men at my workplace. We applied for immigration to Canada as a family.

It took many months and many visits to various department offices in Braunschweig and Hannover before we were given approval. My mother knew of our plans, but we did not inform Heinz's parents for fear of his mother's reaction. We had to be cleared by the health department, had to go through a so-called denazification process, prove at some interviews at the Canadian embassy that we spoke at least some basic English, and most of all, prove that we had a sponsor. By this time, Juergen's year at the farm was almost up and since the Sagers had come to like and respect him very much, they offered to sponsor us.

We could not have been happier. I resigned from the *Kripo* as of December 31, 1953. By the middle of February we began selling our furniture, which really consisted only of a double bed, a wardrobe and a few chairs, and moved in with my mother for the last two weeks before our departure. We had saved up enough money to pay for our passage by boat, and had packed our belongings, including some dishes, pots, pans and bedding into two large wooden crates, and addressed them to Sager's farm.

As Juergen and I had done in Thurow, I promised our mother that we would bring her over to Canada to live with us as soon as we had established ourselves and found a place of our own to live. Unfortunately the relationship between us and Heinz's parents had deteriorated again over the last year. I still tried to be social and polite to his mother and sometimes talked to his father, but they did not want to have anything to do with Heinz and he not with them. They did not find out that we were about to leave Germany until about two weeks before our departure, when our furniture was taken out of the house. We actually were glad, not having told them before this, because it caused a terrific scene with Heinz's mother, who tried to make us feel guilty and refused to say goodbye to us.

•

ON TUESDAY, MARCH 2, 1954, we left Salzgitter-Bad by train at 8 o'clock in the morning with baby and one suitcase, which is still in Gert's possession. Our destination was Bremerhaven. We had our tickets for the ship, *Gripsholm*, from Norddeutscher Lloyd, and train tickets from Halifax to Kitchener which Juergen had bought and sent to us. For five days we were delayed in Bremerhaven, camping out with hundreds of other immigrants in a huge hangar and waiting for the ship to get ready. I started a letter to my mother, to which I added my impressions each day and which I finally sent to her from Troy. She saved it, and I translated it much later, as follows:

Voyage Diary: Bremerhaven, Wednesday, March 3, 1954—Day 2

Dear Muettlein! So far the whole junior Klassen family loves this trip. We hope that you are not sad and depressed. We are all fine and you now can have a quiet time to yourself. If it gets too quiet for you turn up the radio so that people in the street can hear it.

Today we already had a lot of new experiences, most of all *Gertchen*.[1] The night in the large waiting hall was less comfortable, the other women talked until 12 o'clock at night and kept the lights on. The men slept in a different hall. I set up our umbrella in front of Gert and me. He fell asleep right away but it was already 8 p.m. Everything was very primitive but, thank God, it wasn't for long. At 3:30 the first woman got up—of course that woke everybody else up. I didn't sleep very much anyway because I was afraid that Gert might fall out of his bed. It stood next to mine but on the other side was a walkway through the middle of the room. A three-year-old child fell out and screamed. Gert woke up at 4 a.m. and stayed awake until 3 in the afternoon. He was absolutely beat.

We are now on the ship and he is sleeping in his little bed in our tiny cabin. The noise of the motors does not seem to bother him, it really isn't all that bad, just very monotone. We are on a lower deck and unfortunately have no window in the cabin.

At a quarter-to-five this morning we received our breakfast: two buns, a slice of bread, an egg, jam and coffee and milk.

At 6:40 a.m. we left the hall and were taken to the harbour by train in second-class coaches. After many stops we arrived at 9:20 at the Columbus Quay in Bremerhaven. There again everyone waited in huge hangers until we were herded through a customs control where our immunization papers were checked. More waiting. Then a nurse appeared who called all mothers with young children to come on board. The fathers were allowed to come along. This way we were almost the first passengers on board and had lots of time to unpack some of our things.

---

1   Diminutive.

Our two suitcases and the duffel bag were already in the cabin when we arrived; all we had to carry ourselves was the hand luggage.

Gert did not want to leave the ship's rail. There was so much to see! He and Hein[2] were interviewed by a reporter from the *Westfalen Zeitung* in Bielefeld. You may want to write to them for a copy. At 2 o'clock sharp the ship started moving. One hour earlier, the ship's band had already started playing marches and folk songs and Gert was getting his second wind. He was especially interested in the large cranes and he liked the seagulls too. Many visitors had accompanied their departing relatives on board but we were glad that we were alone. They all had to leave the ship an hour before it left the harbour and then just stood behind a high wire fence looking at each other. There was no way they could talk to each other any more, even shouting did not work. At the end the band played *Muss I denn zum Staedtele hinaus* and *Nun ade du mein lieb Heimatland* and *Auf Wiederseh'n*, everybody was moved and many people cried. I didn't, I was excited and ready for the big new adventure.

Today is March 4th. The food here is fantastic. At 4 p.m. they serve coffee and cake and at 10 p.m. again open sandwiches. There is fruit in baskets at every meal, each meal has five courses and even from those you have a choice. We don't even have to fill our plates, the waiters do that for us. Gert eats and eats, he wants something of everything. Our cabin is very small, in the plans it looked fancier. The armchairs all seem to be quite old, only the dancehall on our deck is very pretty and modern. That is also the room in which the meals are served. I guess there is not enough room in the dining hall.

Gertchen entertains all the passengers. When he is finished eating he dances Samba in the middle of the room or he checks out what the other people are eating. His bed is very short, he has to sleep in it diagonally, but he sleeps just fine. Above each of our beds is a lamp and another one above the sink. Since last night the sea has been quite rough and some people are seasick already. Up until now all three of us are okay. I am writing this in the always-busy lounge, it's not quite as shaky here. They

2   Conversational for Heinz.

even have free stationery, and the next letter will be on one of those. Hein and Gert are on deck above. It rains cats and dogs, you can hardly see anything. Tomorrow the ship is supposed to stop in Goeteburg, Sweden, not in Copenhagen as originally planned.

The playroom for the children is not very impressive. We haven't taken Gert there yet, there are so many kids there and they all put the toys in their mouths and have dirty hands. The hobby horse is broken and can't be used. Breakfast is at 7:30, lunch at 12:00 and dinner at 6 o'clock. I can hear Gert calling me, I better stop now. Hein looks exhausted.

Sunday, March 7th—Day 6

After a few days of bad seasickness I am able to write again. The last two days I thought I'd die. Father had to look after the "household". One day Gert started to be sick, too, all over dad's suit, but now he is fine again. He runs and plays, though today he can't run too fast because the "barge" rolls from right to left and back again without stopping. The waves don't look all that high, only a wind force of six, they say.

Since yesterday we are on the Atlantic Ocean. Hein eats so much that he has a constant stomach ache. I must say, though, that they really have the most delicious food and each day you can choose ice cream or fruit or pudding. I have never seen so many types of fruit. Today I was able to eat again. Gert is quite picky, first he wants some of everything and then he spits it out. Only the pudding he gobbles up like a hungry wolf. Last night they showed a movie with Luise Ulrich, too bad I couldn't go.

Last Thursday in the harbour of Goeteburg we danced in the ballroom. At the moment we are sitting in the music salon. The ship's band gives daily concerts—one hour in the morning and one in the afternoon. As of yesterday the sun is shining again. We are mostly sitting on deck in wicker chairs with blankets around us. Gert sits still when I sing to him, he wants me to do that all the time. The tourist deck apparently is overbooked. They had to clean out some storage rooms to put some people in there. There are only 36 people in first class. We were told that there had been only two on the previous crossing. On deck we can play table tennis and some other games, inside is a large store with everything you want. We can pay everything in Deutsche Marks—the money exchange will take place in Halifax.

Gert said a few times: *"Hause gehen, Bus kommt"* (Let's go home, bus is coming), but he likes the water. He always imitates the seagulls. Today at dinner the ship shook so much that all plates slid off the tables. Gert thought it was hilarious! Thank goodness our plates were already empty.

The ship's passengers are almost all immigrants. Most are from southern Germany but there are also quite a few English families. In Goeteburg, another 200 passengers joined us.

Yesterday one of the stewardesses patted Gert's head and he said indignantly, *"rueckt?"* (meaning *verrueckt*: "Are you crazy?") I wonder where he heard that?! He calls the seagulls *"Deiwels"* (devils). That word he probably picked up from me.

Thursday, March 11th—Day 10

Yesterday I was seasick again, wind force of 10.[3] Today it is 11 but strangely enough I am alright. Maybe I'm getting used to the roller coaster ride. The waves look beautiful, they are as high as mountains. Gerti had a bit of a fever, 38.5. A laxative helped. I watched two movies, both English and I did not understand much. Gert now likes it in the playroom but he always plays by himself and only if we stay in the room with him.

They have a tailor on board and you can get your dresses ironed! Every day we get two fresh towels. As of noon today we still have 750 miles to go; on Saturday we are supposed to land in Halifax. Every night is some sort of entertainment, which is very nice. One hundred and ninety-two passengers are booked for Canada, the rest all go to the U.S.A.

By now the noise of the motors gets on my nerves. I will be glad

---

3   Force 10 is defined as very high waves (29-41 feet) with overhanging crests, sea white with densely blown foam, heavy rolling, low visibility. Force 11 is a violent storm. A wind force of 12 is equivalent to a hurricane.

when we finally arrive. We haven't been in the swimming pool yet, the boat is shaking too much. Gert tells me often: *"Omi-Greta-Mama-Omi-nein"*, (meaning that his Omi, my mother, was no longer with us.) It is his way of explaining that he misses you. Often he is very quiet, Hein thinks he is homesick and I believe him.

Halifax: Sunday, March 14th—Day 13

Finally we arrived! Until tonight we had a terrific storm, wind force 12, but we are all okay. Still on board, arrived at 10 a.m., your time 15:00. Beautiful landscape, still a lot of snow and 0 degrees.

Same day. We're in the train now but still standing in Halifax—finally I am sitting at our destination. We ate lunch at 11 o'clock on board the *Gripsholm*. At 12 o'clock, all the Canada-bound passengers left the ship while the band played. Again we had to wait in a huge hall with long benches, but not for a long time. Someone came to inspect our immunization certificates, then we moved to a station where the passports were checked. Lots of forms and paperwork. We then were shown to a wicket where we received our train tickets, which Juergen had arranged. While all this went on the Salvation Army handed out reading material in English and German for the trip.

We then were ushered downstairs into an even larger hall with baggage everywhere. We found our boxes and suitcases under the letter "K", but we did not have to carry them, only the hand luggage. I had to change Gert's pants twice, there was no washroom that I could see far and wide. The crates and suitcases were inspected superficially. Hein said he saw two broken cups. There were no objections and several porters loaded all the luggage onto the special train that was waiting for us. It had blue upholstered seats but no partitions, it looked like a humongous bus. The seats could be rotated and the coaches were numbered for us. There are no other passengers on this train but the immigrants. By 4 p.m. we had found and claimed our seats. There was enough time left for us to return to still another huge hall where we could buy food for the train ride. For $4 we bought a big bag full of good stuff: one loaf of white bread, one rye bread, one jar of strawberry jam, (30 cents), one kilogram of apples (60 cents), one pound of oranges, two bags of cookies, two bags of candies, one tin of meat, one jar of pickles and some cheese. Fresh milk and butter was available on the train. The Salvation Army sold us some stamps. We then sent a telegram to Juergen in Troy: "Arrive Tuesday, 9:25 a.m." (80 cents).

In Montreal and Toronto we have to transfer on our way to Kitchener where Juergen and Mr. Sager will be waiting for us. In Halifax we did not get to see anything. It snowed very heavily and besides my curls would have gone flat. We will leave Halifax at 6 p.m. The train has double windows and it is very hot in here. The last two days on the ship have been awful, even the crew was fed up with the wind. I was again very seasick and for the rest of my life I don't ever again want to have anything to do with the "Christian Seafare". It's either by plane or not at all.

We exchanged 350 DM. For 4.40 DM we received $1. A few minutes ago Hein ripped his pants. A new suit is needed. So far I like everything here. You have to come soon! There will be no trouble with the luggage etc. It is all done for you. On the ship there was an 83 year old Oma who survived the storm better than I did.

The train has hot and cold water and people everywhere seem to use paper towels. The conductor is a black man. Gert was amazed!

Monday, March 15th—Day 14

We survived the night so-so. Gert used up most of the bench space. Everything is still covered with snow. We are travelling now, at 10:45 a.m. past Mont Joli on the St. Lawrence River and are heading toward Quebec City. Just now the sun peeps out and it stopped snowing. The scenery is beautiful, much like the Harz Mountains. The hills are quite high, almost like mountains, all covered with trees in between stretches of flat land with enormous fenced-in meadows. For about one hour we have been riding beside the St. Lawrence River. You can hardly make out the opposite river bank near the horizon. It looks like a big lake. Everywhere along the river bank are fir trees and cedars and little wooden cottages.

The river is to our right and on the left are immediate steep mountains. The communities all look like resorts, beautiful wooden houses with open or glassed-in verandahs. Everything seems to have been built without a plan. In the little villages there is just one road for cars. I haven't seen any other streets. The street lights at night are quite primitive and very dim, like the lanterns we had in Brietzig. All the posts are crooked and bent, just tree trunks from the nearby forests. We haven't seen any small cars yet, just very large and elegant-looking ones. The trucks are also much larger than the ones in Germany.

Between 6 and 8 p.m. tonight we are expected to arrive in Montreal. There we have to transfer. Every few hundred metres or so, it seems, there is a sawmill. The churches are especially pretty, adorned with many decorations and several steeples. The stairs of the houses leading to the upstairs are on the outside instead of inside, it looks very peculiar. Just now we turned our watches back one hour again, that is six hours altogether since we left Germany. It is now 12:45 p.m. and we are still not yet in Quebec City. What a big country! I want Gert to sleep, but he cries without stopping. The sun shines and the snow is melting everywhere.

At 1:30 p.m. we are finally arriving in Quebec City. A peculiar town, with a very primitive station but all around are monumental buildings. One to two metre thick ice floes are floating in the river, a horrific noise from some construction work nearby. The train stopped only for five minutes. Now we are riding through what seems to be a very poor area with only huts as houses. The land is flat, some bush, meadows and forests.

At 7 p.m. we arrived in Montreal. It is a fantastic first impression, with skyscrapers and a high mountain in the background that has a large lit-up cross at the peak. We left Montreal at 8:45 p.m. and arrived in Toronto at 6:10 a.m. Fantastic train station, many shops. Father and son have gone to see if they can buy some stamps. Many good wishes until next time and don't get frightened alone.

Love, Doerte

CHAPTER ELEVEN

Beginning Life in Canada

My first impressions of the new country were overwhelming. Everything seemed to be so different than back home. The train coaches were huge and the cabins upholstered. Everything was large—the cars, the houses and barns we saw from the train. The fields and forests seemed to go on without end. Never had I seen as big and wide a river as the St. Lawrence, not to mention the enormous ice floes that jammed into each other on the water. The advertising billboards around the Toronto train station were huge and one read "Dove", which made me laugh. I wondered what it meant, because that expression as I read it with my German vocabulary, meant "stupid".

It was enroute that we discovered we would have to disembark in Toronto, as our "immigrant train" would not be stopping in Kitchener. We did not concern ourselves too much with this news, believing that Juergen and the Sagers, in this land of endless possibilities, would know this, and would be expecting us in Toronto.

We waited and waited for Juergen to arrive, but after a few hours, Heinz decided to find a telephone to call the Sagers. As it turned out, he and Mr. Sager had not been all-knowing after all, and had driven to Kitchener, expecting us to arrive there. By about mid-day, they finally arrived in Toronto to pick us up, and our new life in Canada officially began.

I am not quite sure what I had expected Ontario to look like but I remember thinking while we were driving to Troy that this landscape could very well have been in Germany. Mrs. Sager welcomed us with open arms; she was an extremely kind and friendly woman and made me feel very comfortable right away. I only wished I could have understood what everyone was saying to us. There were so many questions I wanted to ask and I realized that they asked questions of me which I did not know how to answer.

I remember that I was awed by the beautiful house in which they lived. The kitchen alone was as big as the whole flat from which we had come. It had a washing machine and a large refrigerator, the fridge being a thing I had never heard of before. Every room was at least as large as the kitchen and had beautiful antique furniture in each. To the bedrooms upstairs led a wide, carpeted winding staircase, just as I had seen in the movies, and we were assigned to a large bright room with a humongous bed in the middle and a small bed for our baby. Here I also saw for the first time built-in closets, which impressed me because it seemed to save a lot of space.

Mrs. Sager was an excellent cook. The quality, and even more so the quantity, of the food surprised me at each meal. One morning she served us half a grapefruit, which I did not know, but liked. Other foods that were strange to me were broccoli, green asparagus, celery stalks and corn. At home, corn was fed to the animals, so at first, I was very reluctant to even try it.

Mr. and Mrs. Sager lived in one side of the house while their son, Stanton, and his wife Joan, both in their early 20s, lived in the other half. The young couple did not talk to us much and made no efforts to be friendly. I suppose they were just shy and did not know what to make of these strangers who had arrived at their doorstep. To get to our bedroom I had to pass by the bedroom of the young Sagers. They always left their door open and I was amazed and appalled at the unbelievable disorder in their room. [1]

While I tried to make myself useful in the house, Heinz went with Mr. Sager and Juergen to help outside and in the barn. They had quite a lot of milk cows that were all on automatic milking machines—also something I had never seen before. The strangest thing of all was that there really was always a radio playing music in the barn. Mr. Sager said that the cows liked it and gave more milk.

After three days, Heinz asked Mr. Sager to take him to Kitchener because he wanted to look for a job. Heinz stayed somewhere in Kitchener for several days while Gert and I remained with the Sagers in Troy. He found an immigration agency and a German lady who worked there assigned us a room in a house on King Street.

After a week at Sager's place, the three of us moved to Kitchener. When we arrived there after the first 10 days in Canada, I realized that the accommodation Heinz had found for us was a shelter for new arrivals from Germany. Each of the five or six rooms in the house was occupied by a German family and all shared the same kitchen and the same bathroom. There were a lot of children, the kitchen was constantly in use by somebody and the noise in the place was bothering me a lot. Heinz went out every morning to look for work and after about a week or so he found something. By now I have forgotten what type of work it was, but at the time it did not matter anyway; all we wanted to do was get a place of our own and leave that noisy and not very clean house.

We found a very small flat on Agnes Street in an addition to a private

---

1   Lawrence Sager died in the 1960s. He was still quite young, between 50 and 60 years old. Their only son, Stanton, who was married and had one daughter, did not like farm work, although the farm had been in the family since the early 1700s. He neglected his duties and within a few years the farm became completely run-down despite Mrs. Sager's efforts to hold things together. Eventually she disinherited her son and sold all the land but stayed for several years in the beautiful old farmhouse. When that became too much for her, she moved to Brantford into an apartment. She remarried when she was 90 to a 65 year old man. They had four years together, when he died of a heart attack. She lived to the age of 96. Her son and his wife had gotten a divorce. Mrs. Sager cut him out of her Will altogether, and left her considerable inheritance to her granddaughter.

house, that consisted of one small living-bedroom, a smaller kitchenette and an even smaller bathroom. We rented it for $12 per week. Since we did not have a bed—just a double pull-out sofa—our poor little boy had to sleep for about a week in the bathtub until we managed to find a small bed for him at the Salvation Army furniture store. Heinz had the chance to work overtime and when he was lucky, he could make $10 a day, which was a lot of money for us.

Not far from our flat was a supermarket. I remember the first time I went to shop there I was completely overwhelmed by all the food that was available and by the low prices of everything. A loaf of bread cost 10 cents, a dozen eggs 15 cents (while we had to pay 60 pennies for one egg in Germany—about the same as an entire dozen cost here), a pound of butter 30 cents, and so on. When I think back now, I am sure that the supermarket was nothing compared to the size of a supermarket today, but at the time I had never before seen food in such quantity and such variety.

Right away I bought coffee, sugar, chocolate, puddings and whatever else I thought my mother in Germany would have difficulty getting and made up a parcel for her in the way I had been used to sending a parcel back home. I organized wrapping paper and string, took a fountain pen, white paper and glue for the address and stuffed all the treasure into a cardboard box.

With all this under my arm and little Gert by my side I walked to the nearest post office and presented the contents of the box with a prepared list to the man behind the counter. As I began to unpack each item to show him what I intended to send he looked at me strangely and started talking to me in a waterfall of words, of which I did not understand a single one. People behind me began to laugh and when he started throwing all my bags and packages back in the large box I realized to my amazement that here in Canada you did not have to account for what you sent away and there were no restrictions on either items nor amounts of goods. It took me awhile to properly pack, wrap and address the parcel but when it was done he took it without question and sent it on its way. I thought: "What a wonderful and free country!"

It certainly was not easy to function in a strange country with a language that was foreign to me. Before I left Germany I did not worry too much about it because I had had eight years of school-English and thought that I would get by. But being here, the people spoke very fast and it seemed with a different dialect than the one I had learned in school. The worst thing was that I first had to translate everything in my head before it made sense to me. Of course, by the time I managed to translate one little thing, people had said four or five other things already. The language might as well have been Chinese; it went by my ears like a crash, just one big noisy sound. If I tried to answer, I had to go through the same translation procedure and it always took much too long.

Because of this language difficulty several funny things happened. I remember riding the public transportation bus in Kitchener for the first time. I had noticed that people entered at the front and always left through the middle doors, so I worked my way to the middle and when the bus stopped where I wanted to get off, the doors did not open. I became frantic and the people realized that I wanted to get off and shouted something at me. Suddenly somebody gave me a push and I stepped forward on the step and voila! The doors opened.

Only then did I realize that the people had said: "Step down!" The next time I knew.

Another time I took a walk with Gert and we came by a construction site where some big machines were being used. We stopped to look at them and I explained to Gert in German: look at this big *Bagger*. A bagger in German means an earth-moving machine; it is spelled with "a" but pronounced as "u". A woman walked by and gave me a very dirty look. She was probably wondering what kind of language I was teaching that little boy.

We were always surprised to see so few people walking on the streets. Nobody but us seemed to take, for instance, an evening or Sunday afternoon stroll. All those cars were an unusual sight for us and often we thought that it would be nice if we could afford a car as well. But for the time being we had no complaints and were quite satisfied with the way things had gone so far.

I had always been ambitious and viewed our little flat as very temporary. I decided that I needed a job and found one very soon in a restaurant as dishwasher during evening hours when Heinz was home with Gert. At that time there were no automatic dishwashers and every plate and glass had to be washed by hand. It did not take long until my hands were raw and blistered from the strong detergents. Nobody had offered me gloves and it did not occur to me that there were such things as rubber gloves. I lasted about three or four weeks before I had to quit.

We stayed for the rest of that first summer in Kitchener, took many pictures and I wrote many letters home about all the new impressions and experiences.

Tavistock

AT ONE TIME, I REMEMBER, we met a very nice older German lady who wanted to rent her house to us. We were delighted and had made arrangements to move in there but by the end of the summer Heinz met a young German man by the name of Schaffhausen who had started a carpentry business in Tavistock. He and his wife and son had lived with a German Lutheran Minister, but were preparing to move out into a small house of their own.

The minister, Pastor Stockmann, was now looking for a new housekeeper and Schaffhausen needed a helper in his new business. We decided that we qualified. Schaffhausen took us for an introductory meeting to Tavistock and by the end of August, Heinz and I had a new place to live in a huge old house which seemed to me like a mansion. It was surrounded by a very large garden. In it grew many flowers, berries of all kinds and many vegetables. Pastor Stockmann, who was about 75 years old at that time, paid me $1 per day and for that I kept house and cooked for him as well as for ourselves. We did not have to pay any rent. He also owned several dozen capons and each Sunday he killed one, which I then had to prepare and cook. Shortly after we moved in he bought two bushels of peaches which I had to preserve in jars. There were over 40 of them. From his house to the village and the nearest store was at least a good mile for me to walk. Gert's little legs often got tired and carrying him as well as the groceries was not always easy.

Several times we received visitors from Pastor Stockmann's family. He had seven married children and was a grandfather many times over. I always tried to be the perfect hostess and would cook, bake and clean before their arrival until late into the night. One of his sons owned a cheese factory near Woodstock and a few times we visited there. Of course, we did not have a car and were totally dependent on our pastor if it came to leaving Tavistock. I got along very well with him. Heinz, however, often argued with him. They both were quite bossy and stubborn and that always put me in a very uncomfortable position in the middle.

Since we, as well as Schaffhausens all spoke German, my English did not improve very much. Sometimes I asked Pastor Stockmann for phrases or newspaper translations and tried to read as many English articles and papers as I had time to do, always with a dictionary beside me.

Once a couple came to the door when I was alone in the house. They wanted to see the pastor. I told them, he had gone to a funeral, pronouncing the "u" as in the word "fun". It was very difficult for me to tell, which vowels were to be pronounced short and which ones long. Only many years later, when I attended Teachers' College in Toronto did I learn the grammatical rules.

On September 4, 1954, Juergen married his long-time girlfriend, Anne Klatt. He had moved to Toronto after his work at Sager's came to an end in the spring, and found a job and a furnished room. Anne lived with her married sister, Lydia, and worked as a bank teller for the Bank of Montreal. Their marriage took place in Tavistock with Pastor Stockmann as the celebrating minister, Lydia and myself being the bridesmaids, and Heinz being the best man. Mr. and Mrs. Sager and Pastor Stockmann had greatly helped me with the planning of this momentous event and Anne's father and uncle who attended, having arrived from Pittsburg, bore most of the expenses. The church women's group cooked a delicious turkey dinner, followed by a big wedding cake, and festivities took place in the St. Sebastian church hall. Mr. and Mrs. Sager were the guests of honour and during the church service we played on a record player a German hymn that my mother sang, and had shipped to me in lieu of her presence. This again had to be a great sacrifice on her part, not being able to attend the wedding of her only son.

During the summer I realized that we were going to have another baby early in the new year of 1955. It was a very easy pregnancy but Pastor Stockmann insisted that I should see the doctor in the village, a Dr. Fisher. We lived a very healthy lifestyle, our food was mostly grown in the garden or bought at some farm. I had lots of "exercise", looking after house and garden and our little Gert, who loved the place and at least once a week walked with me to the village to get some groceries or stamps from the post office. It was no wonder that our new baby arrived as a healthy big boy of about 10 pounds. This event happened on February 17th at 11:55 a.m. in the hospital in Stratford where Pastor Stockmann had driven me early in the morning. We had made arrangements with Lydia, Juergen's wife's sister, in Toronto, to take Gert for the time of my hospital confinement, and Heinz took him on this day by train to Toronto to her and her family. I was very concerned and worried about him since he had never been away from us, and rightly so. He was very unhappy during these days as we found out later.

We named our new little boy "Roland Heinz Juergen", but to this day I always call him Roli. To my great surprise, I received many cards and even gifts from women in the congregation who had seen us on Sundays in church. After a week Heinz brought Gert back. They came to the hospital and the children and I left with the family of Pastor Stockmann's oldest son, who was also a minister, and who had invited the three of us to stay with them for a week until I became a little stronger again. I remember how grateful and happy I was there and how impressed I was about the friendliness and hospitality of the Canadian people. I knew quite definitely that we had made the right decision to come to Canada.

Life in Tavistock, however, became a little more stressful during the next few months.

Heinz lost his job with Schaffhausen, who had decided to move to Florida with his family, and eventually found a packer's job in a box factory for 60 cents per hour. In addition to that he and the pastor became more and more irritated with each other and I had my work cut out with the two small children. Our bedroom was on the second floor where the baby slept, too far away for me to hear him downstairs. I was constantly running up and down the stairs to check on him, at the same time paying enough attention to Gerti, who began to become upset about this new intruder. The shopping in the village became a real challenge. I now had to push the baby carriage we had acquired on the sidewalk through the snow, and poor little Gert got tired marching in boots and snowsuit one mile there and one mile back.

Moving to Toronto

FINALLY SPRING ARRIVED, and one day in early May, 1955, Heinz decided to take the train to Toronto to look for a job. After three days he arrived back with the news that he had found a job with the company "Fruehauf Trailer", and that he also had rented an apartment, to be moved into in two weeks.

As it turned out, the story about the apartment was correct, but he had not found a job. He was just very anxious to get out of Tavistock and was sure to find some work once we lived in the city. In many ways I felt sorry to leave the pastor and the big old mansion with the beautiful garden, but on the other hand I was extremely excited to finally have a home for ourselves and saw, as Heinz did, the greater potential for us in a large city. Pastor Stockmann was very kind to us and gave us several pieces of furniture, a bed, a sofa, chairs, a chest of drawers, a table and lots of preserves from the previous fall.

We rented a truck and transported ourselves and our belongings to No. 20 Greentree Court, near Eglinton and Keele Streets in North York, Toronto. Juergen, now a married man living in Toronto, helped to carry the furniture up to the fourth floor. There was no elevator in the building. I was more than happy, having such a big apartment! It consisted of a living room, a bedroom and a very small kitchen and bathroom, but to me it appeared huge compared to what we had been used to in Germany.

The rent was $ 90 per month, which was a lot. We were able to sell our Leica camera for a few hundred dollars which gave us a few months rent.

After about a week of job hunting, Heinz found one as tool and dye maker, earning 80 cents an hour. We became friends with a young English couple, the Woods, who lived in the next block. They already owned a car and twice took us out on a Sunday. The first time we went north to one of the many lakes and the second time I had no idea where we were going, even though they kept telling me the name of the place. To my utter surprise I noticed on the way the signs that pointed in the direction of Niagara Falls, and I finally realized that I had not understood their pronunciation of the word. Of course, I could read it now. My excitement grew with every minute. I remembered that even in school I had always wanted to see the wonders of the world and Niagara Falls was definitely one of them. Never will I forget the first gigantic impression that I had when I saw the Falls. I stood there awestruck and thought about the little village of Brietzig from which I had come and which now lay so far away on a different continent, and again contemplated the wondrous directions life can take. It seemed as if I had appeared here in a different incarnation, and gratefulness and zest for life filled me to overflowing.

Unfortunately, Heinz's job ended after five or six weeks, and we were desperately in need of an income.

Two Income Household

I DECIDED THAT I WAS GOING to look for work as well, and followed some advertisements in the paper. The first one I went to was a cookie factory on the outskirts of the city, meaning that I had to take three buses and then still walk 15 minutes to get there. The job paid 65 cents an hour. It did not take me long to decide that this was not worth my while. It was way too far from home and while I was gone I had to pay a babysitter. So I became a babysitter myself for several weeks to a little girl whose mother lived in our building, She paid me $3 a week, which I saved, and then bought an old typewriter for $15. That was a big improvement to my life. Now I could type all the many letters that I wrote home and save much time doing so. Then someone told me about a meat packing factory, Canada Packers, which apparently paid good wages and always needed help. I did go to apply, had to complete a speed test with my hands and was hired on the spot for $1.15 an hour! What luck! What elation!

There was only one fly in the ointment: I had to work the afternoon shift from 4 p.m. to midnight. However, on the same day I found a young woman with two small children who lived in the same building and who was willing to babysit for me. For a few days Heinz went out in the morning to look for work and then stayed with the children in the afternoon. Soon he had found a day job at the Rothmans cigarette factory, as maintenance man with improved wages, and came home every day at 5 p.m.

This meant the children only had to be with the babysitter for one-and-a-half hours, since I left at 3:30. At first it was very hard for all of us. I felt terrible, having to leave my little boys with a strange woman. But she seemed nice and having small children herself, my two had company to play with.

On my arrival at work on the first day I was handed a white smock and a thick white overcoat against the cold. Then someone instructed me in the method of punching the clock in and out, showed me a locker and the lunchroom, and placed me in front of a meat slicing machine. There were about 20 young women working in the large room on many different machines, most of them cutting large hams into slices and packages. My machine was cutting four or five foot-long bologna sausages into six or eight or 16-ounce piles. It was my job to regulate the correct weight, adding a slice or taking a piece out, then placing the two piles from the scales on a conveyor belt at the same time.

My co-worker next to me was a Scottish woman who swore like a trooper. At first I was always looking for the blood on the bologna because she constantly called it "bloody bologna". Most of the girls were German and my English vocabulary did not improve a lot.

After several months I was teamed up with a young Polish woman,

Sophie Samulski. We were stationed in a small room with just one cutting machine and four scales, two for each of us. A conveyor belt between our two machines would transport and wrap the cut slices to a table behind us, where another girl packed the ready-to-sell packages in boxes.

Sophie and I soon became good friends, and our friendship has survived throughout our lives. Sophie had been sent as a 12 year old to Germany during the war, and there had worked as a housemaid. In 1950, she immigrated to Canada where she met her future husband, who had lived through several years in a concentration camp as the sole survivor of his family. He died very young, leaving Sophie and three children behind.

The work was extremely boring and I often felt that it was a wasted life. However, the money increased and we were able to pay our bills. Heinz now worked with a man from England whom he liked. He and his wife, Frank and Muriel Culshaw, became good friends of ours for many years until they moved out of Toronto and we lost touch with them, except for occasional contact. While they lived in Toronto, we often visited each other with the children; they also had two sons, and I learned quite a bit of the language from Muriel. Frank played Santa Claus for our two little boys at Christmas in 1955 and '56. Gert recited a German poem and Roli pulled his beard. Juergen and Anne had managed with the financial help of Anne's uncle to buy a lot and to start building their own house. At first Heinz helped them in all his free time for $1 an hour in wages. But after several weeks the two got into an argument and Heinz quit. This put me again in the middle, but I refused to alienate Juergen and Anne. Eventually Heinz came around again and the two acted in a civilized manner with each other, though they never became friends. The house on Willard Gardens was finished in the summer of 1957.

During our first year in Toronto, I had ample opportunity to become acquainted with several local activities in this culture that seemed rather alien to me. I remember my utter surprise to read one day above a door on Eglinton Avenue: "Men Only", and a few yards further down, above another door: "Women and Escorts". I could not believe our apartment was located in the same neighbourhood as a brothel.

It was Muriel who enlightened me at our next visit about the meaning of these signs. She explained that they indicated a bar or restaurant where alcohol was served. At that time, in the 1950s, ladies without the accompaniment of a man were not served alcoholic beverages, and may have been viewed as engaging in questionable moral behaviour. Ironically, an escort today has often come to mean exactly that.

At the end of October I noticed one day that the music on the radio became very wild and weird, to the extent that I shut it off. I usually liked to listen and tried to understand the meaning of the lyrics in the songs. In the late afternoon there was a knock on our door. When I opened it, I saw to my dismay two little boys, aged about eight and nine, standing there in rags, their hair hanging into their faces, holes at the knees of their pants and oversized jackets covering dirty T-shirts. They each carried a basket in which I detected two or three small candy bars. The older boy said something, which I did not understand, but I was certain it was a request to receive something.

My first shocked reaction was, "Do your parents know that you are out begging?" Both boys nodded their heads. I was overcome with pity for them, and disgust for their parents who had obviously sent these two poor little boys out to beg from door to door. It also seemed unbelievable to me how people could have given them some candy bars when it was obvious that they were extremely poor and were probably hungry.

I told them to wait and went into the kitchen where I prepared several peanut butter sandwiches and a piece of Polish sausage for them. I dismissed them with the stern advice to go home and never go begging again. It took another year before I came to understand that this event had happened at Hallowe'en, and that these children had worn costumes, as is the custom for that day.

Omi Hartmann Arrives

EVER SINCE WE HAD ARRIVED in Toronto I had been contemplating how to get my mother to come to Canada. Neither Juergen nor we had enough money to pay her travelling fee and we hoped that she could fly instead of having to endure a long ocean crossing. In 1956 she surprised us with the news that she had enough money saved from her pension and from selling her belongings, that she could afford the flight herself. I was extremely happy at the prospect of seeing her again soon. Before she left Germany, she visited all our relatives one more time. The Berlin contingent accompanied her to the airport on December 17, 1956, and all of us picked her up on the same afternoon at Toronto's Malton Airport. What a happy reunion that was! Juergen and Anne gave her a room in their new house and we saw each other often.

Our first Christmas together, 1956, was of very special significance. We celebrated Christmas Eve gratefully in our apartment, and Christmas Day in Juergen's brand new house, remembering with amazement our life's journey to this time and place. I am still grateful that my mother lived long enough to see both her children settled in their own comfortable homes.

CHAPTER TWELVE

Settlers in Toronto

By the spring of 1957, Heinz and I had saved enough money for a small down payment on a house. We had $500 in a savings account and started to look at houses with a real estate agent to whom we had been introduced by Frank and Muriel. I remember two or three houses in the older part of Toronto. They were all very close to the neighbouring buildings with just a walkway between them, and though the main floors were passable, the basements were smelly, dingy and had dirt floors. I could not see us bringing up two children in neighbourhoods like that and we began to consider moving to the outskirts of Toronto.

Again Frank and Muriel helped us to look and in the spring of 1957 we had found our dream home at 33 Zorra Street in Etobicoke to the west of Toronto. It had been a former farmhouse, had a lovely front and backyard with a lilac hedge and several trees, and most of all it was clean, spacious and the cellar had a cement floor. It seemed a long distance away from the city of Toronto. Except for a few houses on the street and a candy factory across from us, there were only large fields and an apple orchard. However, a bus stop had already been established at the top of our little dead-end street, and we were assured that a school would soon be built within walking distance of our house.

In April, we moved our few belongings into our new $14,000 house. There were two mortgages on the property and we had to come up with a down payment of $2,000, which we did not have. Juergen was kind enough to lend us $1,500, and with our saved $500 the deal could be closed. We had made it! Our very own house! Who cared that there was no furniture to speak of? Heinz and I slept in the living room on the couch that Pastor Stockmann had given us, and the boys slept in the double bed that also originated in Tavistock. In addition, we owned a chest of drawers, a kitchen table and four chairs, and the former owners had left us their gas stove. Clothes could conveniently be hung and placed on shelves in the built-in closets, which were a real blessing and a new experience for us.

The two official mortgage payments were to be made monthly in small amounts but our first effort was to pay back Juergen's loan, which we managed within a year. The second mortgage took longer, and I finally paid off the first mortgage in 1968 after Heinz left. It was only then that I learned to my dismay how mortgages were arranged and how interest was calculated. In the end, we probably paid close to $30,000 for our $14,000 home. But even now I am not sorry that we started in such an ignorant way. We lived in the house for 22 years, and it became the stable home for the children and for me.

The first dinner guests in our new house were Frank and Muriel. Since I still felt rather inferior to them due to my limited command of English, I was quite nervous and spent hours before their arrival in the kitchen cooking to produce the best meal possible.

Once everyone had taken their seat at the table, I continued to find reasons to improve matters in the kitchen. I heard Muriel call out to me to come and take part in the delicious dinner. My answer was, "Oh, it's alright, I am fed up already." There was a silent moment at the table. I realized that I must have made a grave mistake but I did not know what. There was nothing for me to do but join the group and keep my mouth shut while we all ate and the conversation slowly began to pick up again.

Muriel was a gracious and understanding guest. She helped me to clear the table and quietly explained to me the meaning of the words "fed up", whereupon I felt secure enough to explain that I had meant to indicate I was not all that hungry because I had done extensive tasting while preparing the meal. The incident ended with a laugh and more determination in my mind to intensify my study of the language.

From the time of our move from the apartment at Greentree Court to Zorra Street, my daily commute to work at Canada Packers on St. Clair Avenue took much longer than before. I now had to take two busses and a streetcar, which not only took more time but also was more costly. By now I had made peace with the transportation company and the raised bus ticket prices.[1]

During the month of August 1958, we decided that our mother needed a holiday and arranged for her to attend a so-called summer camp in the Muskokas, which happened to be run by a group of Estonians. Her excitement and joy at this time is expressed in a letter she sent home to her friends in Germany, and probably became the highlight of her life in Canada.[2]

My mother, who had a room in Juergen's house, came daily by bus and streetcar and stayed with the boys after I left for work until Heinz came home. She was a wonderful grandmother to my children. Eventually we bought a bed for her and she often stayed a few days with us, which gave me some extra time to catch up on much needed sleep in the morning. However, to this day I feel regret for not having spent more personal time with her, and having taken advantage of her loving kindness and fading energy.

In the summer of 1958 we bought our first car. It was old, huge, green in colour and cost $100.[3] In order to afford this and other "necessities" I had begun to sell Avon products at work during the breaks to my co-workers. This turned out to be a lucrative business, as I earned 33 cents

---

1   At the beginning of my work at the meat packing factory in April 1956, I had to pay five cents for a one-way bus ticket, which also included one transfer. A year later, the price went up to 10 cents, which outraged me to no end because it was a 100 percent increase. For three months I had boycotted the bus company and walked to work every day.

2   The letter was returned to me after her death, by her sister in Berlin.

3   It was a 1949 Mercury.

on every dollar, and with a lot of extra effort, I soon had a growing savings account. Since gasoline was very cheap, we took many weekend trips, which included my mother, into the northern cottage areas. Soon I discovered that many properties by the lakes were for sale and convinced Heinz to at least look at some of these advertised places. One weekend we were shown a peninsula property on Lake Chemung near Peterborough, which looked like a jungle but had great potential. It was listed for $3,000 with the promise of having a simple cottage built on the lot.

I almost went hysterical with excitement, and after much debate we managed to come up with a down payment of $350 from my Avon savings and part of my mother's pension savings, which she generously offered. Now we not only owned a house and a car, but also a cottage!

This really was a wonderful country and I was only too willing to work as hard and as much as I could, including many nightly overtime hours at Canada Packers, when the wages were time-and-a-half. Life was wonderful; we all were young and healthy, and grateful for each opportunity.

But fate struck in October 1958, when one weekend at the cottage, which still was unfinished inside, my mother fell and hit her head on one of the corners of a two-by-four.

She never recovered. She stayed in bed from the time we came back home, and rapidly became weaker and frailer. I tried desperately to find a doctor who would come to see her. My English was still not very good; I just kept calling doctors whose names I found in the phone book but no one was willing to make a house call. Finally one day I spoke to a doctor who agreed to come, but I found out weeks later that he was a chiropractor. He brought different medications, told me what to give her to eat and checked on her once a week, but did not speak very hopefully about her prospects for recovery.

By Christmas, things had gone from bad to worse for my poor mother, and also for me. She seemed to have given up hope of ever getting better and I felt helpless and exhausted from overwork and worry. At the beginning of January, Juergen and Anne decided to take her into their new house and give me a break. This was not an easy step for them either, since Anne had just given birth to their first child, Gordon, on

November 4th. She was now on maternity leave from her job as a teller in a large bank downtown. Having a better command of English than I, she found a different doctor who very quickly diagnosed our mother as having liver cancer and had her moved immediately to the North Western Hospital, which no longer exists.

The following two months were heartbreaking and filled with sadness, worry and sleepless nights for all of us. Watching the suffering and deterioration of my mother's health was almost beyond endurance. I visited her almost daily before reporting for work at 4 p.m., feeling extremely guilty for having to bring my two little boys to the babysitter shortly after lunch instead of at 3 o'clock. On one occasion I took Gert with me to see his Omi, but had to hide him behind my skirt in the elevator, because children were not allowed in the hospital.

Not once did my mother complain or show despair in all those weeks; she just smiled at me when I expressed hopeful thoughts of us together for the future. Before she fell into what may have been a drug-induced coma, one of her last wishes was that Juergen and I should always stay close and supportive of each other.

On Wednesday, April 1, 1959, I was paged at work around 6 p.m. with the message to come to the hospital immediately. By the time I arrived there, my mother had passed over to the other side, nine days before her 64th birthday.

It was left to me to arrange for the funeral. Again, I consulted the telephone directory to find the closest funeral home which happened to be at Lake Shore Boulevard near Kipling. With my two boys by my side I took the bus the following day to this dreaded place.

I remember a large room filled with caskets of all types and having to choose one of the cheaper ones because there were other fees to pay, including a grave site at a cemetery. Because of my still-limited English, I followed the kind suggestions of the funeral director. A time was arranged for a service on Saturday, April 4th, to which I called the German Lutheran Pastor whom I had met once in the hospital when he visited my mother. He gave a kind sermon and accompanied us to the cemetery in Clarkson for the burial. The only people attending were Juergen and my family, Anne's sister Lydia, and Frank and Muriel Culshaw.

Eventually Juergen and I shared the cost of erecting a gravestone. I have a deed for the site, and my ashes will be buried there when the time comes. In 1995, I took the ashes of Heinz, the father of my boys, and had them buried there at the foot of the grave.

•

GERT HAS BEEN CALLED GARRETT since the Christmas when he was five years old. The children with whom he played had begun to tease him about his name, calling him a girl because they insisted that "Gert" was the abbreviation of "Gertrude". This was bad enough for our poor little boy with the pretty German boy's name, but the straw that broke the camel's back came at Christmas, when Heinz submitted the names of both children to his company, who planned to have Santa Claus present a gift to each child of the employees.

On the day of the Christmas party, Roland unwrapped a red fire engine, and Gert found a doll's kitchen in his parcel. He cried, felt embarrassed and humiliated—and so did I, in addition to being angry.

The following day I sent off a letter to the registration office in Salzgitter-Bad, where he was born, with the request for a name change to "Garrett". To me, this pronunciation came closest to the name on his birth certificate. It only took a short time before the return answer arrived with the refusal of any change in the first name, but the assurance that a change in the last name could be granted. What stupidity! Warped German bureaucracy! We decided to be our own best judge and henceforth Gert became Garrett. (I was not exactly happy when I read some time later that garret meant a space in the attic, but what was done was done, and Garrett with two "t"s was a perfectly acceptable boy's name in this wonderful country where nobody cared about the spelling of a name.)

My boys were now six and four years old. Garrett had started school at the kindergarten class the previous year and was now finishing Grade 1. In the fall Roland would be enrolled in kindergarten, both attending the new public school. As young as they were, each day they crossed the Queensway, which was the busy main road with regular car and bus traffic. There were neither crossing guards nor traffic lights at the time—eventually there was an unsupervised crosswalk. The only safety they had was to remember the stern instructions to look left and right before crossing any street. They did follow the directions well and I really was never worried about their safety. Sometimes I sent Garrett to the closest Dominion store which was about half a kilometre east on the Queensway on the opposite side of the road. Times were quieter, slower and safer then.

During the same summer of 1959, Heinz's mother visited us. She had taken the sea route to Montreal and had planned to stay for three months. However, after four weeks she decided she had had enough of this country— in which she could not understand anybody but us—and where both Heinz and I were working each day which left her to be the babysitter. She disliked our friends Frank and Muriel, slept in the car when they visited on two occasions, and found it disgusting how older women were dressing themselves in brightly coloured clothing and sometimes even in shorts. Her own dresses were brown, gray or black, which made the humidity and heat difficult for her to tolerate, especially since we did not own an air conditioner. Heinz bought a plane ticket for her, and she and we were happy to see her go.

Every single weekend we drove to our cottage on Lake Chemung, which had become more habitable with the furniture that originated in Tavistock. In time we had been able to buy a new sofa and chair, a dining room and a bedroom set for the house in Etobicoke. The cottage lot had been cleared so that the lake was now visible; fill had been brought in and new trees and grass had been planted. For me, it was a piece of Heaven.

One fishing episode turned out to be traumatic, when Heinz and the two boys went on the lake in a rowboat and the hook of Heinz's fishing line caught Roli's ear as Heinz snapped back his rod to make a cast. Because the hook was barbed it was not easily removed, and to get help they first had to row back from the middle of the lake. It was a Sunday afternoon and the first attempt to find a doctor in the nearest village of Bridgenorth was unsuccessful. Finally Heinz took Roland to the emergency at the hospital in Peterborough while I "freaked out" with worry at the cottage, where he had ordered me to stay with Garrett. The hook was successfully removed with the help of a pair of pliers and Roli did get rid of his unwanted ear decoration. He was still too young for a body piercing.

Another memorable cottage episode happened to me one day when I was standing on a wooden stepladder, painting the side of the cottage. I decided that I needed a short break to get a drink of juice, climbed down and was just turning around the corner about three metres away from the ladder, when suddenly with a tremendous noise, a branch, about 18 inches thick, came crushing down from a very old birch tree overhead. It hit the ladder straight on and splintered it into innumerable pieces. My Guardian Angel certainly had been on standby—again! Had I hesitated only several seconds more on that ladder, I would not be here to tell the tale.

Frank and Muriel visited several times on Sunday afternoons and so did Juergen and Anne, but other than that, Heinz did not like anyone to come. During one summer holiday the nine-year-old daughter of my friend, Sophie, with whom I worked at Canada Packers, stayed with us for a week. She had much fun with our boys arranging turtle races, catching chipmunks and exploring the wilderness.

During the week, life went on as usual with both boys going to school in the mornings. Heinz worked the day shift at the chocolate company, Rowntree, and I worked the afternoon shift, from 4 p.m. until midnight, at Canada Packers. Heinz would often pick me up at that time on Fridays, with the boys sleeping in the back seat. We all looked forward to the weekends at the cottage.

CHAPTER THIRTEEN

A Teaching Career

During the latter half of the 1950s, a small Catholic school was built in our neighbourhood, on Islington Avenue, which also served on Sundays as substitute church. In the fall of 1961, we transferred our two boys from the public school into this new school—Holy Angels. Garrett attended Grade 4 and Roland, Grade 2. After about two months I went to the school one morning to check out what was being taught there. What I heard in Grade 2 satisfied me, however, the Grade 4 teacher did not sound at all acceptable. My decision was immediate: I transferred the children back to their former public school, using as an excuse that the longer daily walk was too much for them.

At just about that time, the congregation decided to build a church for the community. To raise funds, a dinner was organized on a Sunday in May 1961, in which Heinz and I decided to participate. We were seated opposite a friendly woman, who happened to be the wife of the local school board administrator. During our social conversation I mentioned having taught as supply teacher in Germany, and heard from her that her husband frequently was in need of supply teachers. During the afternoon I was introduced to her husband, who requested my address and telephone number, and indicated that he might call me if my services should ever be needed.

My hopes immediately went sky high—here seemed to be an escape route from the daily drudgery and ungodly working hours at the meat packing plant. During the following weeks and months I increased my efforts to become more fluent in English by studying vocabulary books and reading as much as possible.

I waited with great expectation all summer long, but neither a call nor a letter arrived regarding my hopes. Eventually I resigned myself to the thought it was not to be, and was glad that at least I had a well-paying job to go to.

Then, on December 17th of the same year, the phone rang—it was the administrator, whose name has unfortunately disappeared from my memory—asking whether he could come to our home to interview me for a possible teaching position. Of course, I agreed!

He arrived the following day for the interview and after about half-an-hour I was hired for the term from January to June, 1962, as a supply teacher in a Grade 3 class at Holy Angels School in our parish.

With the greatest of pleasure I handed in my resignation at Canada Packers, effective December 31, 1961.

The New School Teacher

AFTER THE CHRISTMAS HOLIDAYS my new life began. Despite my enthusiasm and great intentions, I was very nervous when the principal of the school, Mr. Boulanger, introduced me first to the staff and then to my class of 35 bright-eyed eight-year olds. He had explained that I was taking over a class from a teacher who had moved away and that I would find the necessary books for the different subjects in the classroom. I was also handed a small gray curriculum book which I was to study and follow. No further advice or instructions were given; as in the school years ago, in Germany, I was left to my own devices. I did not even know that daily lesson plans were required. My preparations consisted of copious random notes, and reliance on my memory of my dear old village school teacher's methodology.

The day in my class started with the singing of the National Anthem, a prayer, the inspection of clean hands, eyes, ears and teeth, and the roll call which was followed by the checking of the previously assigned homework. After a day or two I found an old timetable and realized that I had to adhere to a given schedule, and that a specific time was allotted to each subject. Eventually I adjusted the timetable to my own liking.

The secretary requested a seating plan, which also helped me greatly, then handed me a "register". It was a very large hardcover attendance book that had to be kept meticulously every day. It was only with her kind help at the end of the first month that I was able to figure out how to arrive at the various required percentages of attendances and absences.

During the recesses and at lunch, I mostly sat quietly in the staff-room, listening to the talk of the other teachers, trying to learn as much as I could. Many of their words were strange to me, such as "phonics, comprehension, IQ level, integration, short and long vowels", and so on, and this caused me to work at home with the dictionary more than ever. A few select TV programs helped me with the pronunciation. At home, we had begun more and more often to speak in English, mainly because the children frequently started to answer in English instead of German, and their pronunciation was more correct than ours.

One morning in mid-February a gentleman arrived in my class who introduced himself as "the inspector" and, to my surprise, took a seat in the back of the room. As usual, I went through my morning routine and then proceeded with some instruction. When recess time arrived and the children had been dismissed, he sat me down, and in a rather amused way, informed me that in Canada children could not be inspected in regard to their morning hygiene or any other personal health routine. I was also told that shortly I would have to undergo a written and oral test at the office of the Ministry of Education to obtain a temporary teaching certificate.

This day arrived the following week. Together with about two dozen other men and women, I presented myself at the government building, and nervously hoped for the best.

The day began with dictation, followed by an essay about why we wished to become a teacher, and finally, a written mathematics test. By that time we were given a lunch break and in the afternoon each person had to face a committee of seven gentlemen.

When my turn came, I was questioned about my background and previous work experience in Germany, then had to read aloud a paragraph from a book. In doing so, I gave all my concentration to the pronunciation and was unable to answer questions about the content. I had recognized one of the gentlemen around the table as being the inspector who had observed my morning class several days earlier. He now obviously noticed my embarrassment and in a kind voice asked me to re-read the paragraph silently for comprehension, which I did. It was a short story about an entangled bird and my answers probably were passable, though I wished I had done better.

Finally, around 4 p.m., all applicants had been tested. We were told whether we had passed or failed, and—hurray!—I was one of only a handful of people who had made the grade. My position at Holy Angels School was secure until the end of the school year in June. Until then I worked hard at my new occupation. I learned how to prepare better lesson plans, listened to the other teachers on staff, and asked for help and advice, often regarding discipline problems. One Grade 5 teacher in particular was greatly supportive.

The teacher's name was Miss Turner. Most of the help I needed was in the disciplinary area, since some of the children's behaviour was unruly, inattentive and noisy. One girl especially presented much trouble because she never seemed to be able to stay in her seat longer than 10 minutes at a time, and then would proceed to disturb the rest of the class.

After having tried various methods on my own—unsuccessfully—to calm her down, I asked Miss Turner for advice.

She told her own children that they would be getting an addition for the next hour, but wished that no attention should be paid to the newcomer. She then proceeded to quietly take my little troublemaker into her own classroom, after kindly explaining that she would give her the opportunity to move and walk around in her Grade 5 classroom to her heart's content. The only condition to this privilege would be that the girl would have to keep walking around and around, and could not sit down again, until the next bell sounded.

The result of this exercise was amazing. In the future, I only had to point my finger toward the wall of the next classroom, and order was restored.

On Miss Turner's advice, I also involved the parents of certain students which, at the beginning, was an intimidating experience for me because of my inexperience, and what I considered to be my still-limited English language skills. However, it turned out to be a great help for everyone concerned: the children, the parents and not least of all, for me.

Becoming a Student Again

IN JUNE OF 1962 MY SIX MONTHS of temporary teaching were over and I had to face the decision of whether to return to my job at Canada Packers or attend classes at the Teachers' College for at least one year, possibly two, depending on my performance.

In my mind there was only one answer: quit the meat factory and go to college!

This, however, meant that for at least one year we had to live on one income only, and sacrifices had to be made. Heinz was understanding, if not exactly happy, and agreed that I should try my luck with a view to the prospect of a better future in the years to follow.

In order to be accepted as a student at Teachers' College, proof had to be presented of my Grade 13 high school diploma. Since all my papers were lost at the end of the war, my only recourse was to try to find witnesses who could testify on my behalf. With the help of the Red Cross I found the address of my former school friend, Rosi Laaps, who was able to contact two of our former Grade 13 teachers. They, in turn, sent me a notarized declaration stating that I had passed the *Abitur* in the spring of 1943. From Rosi, I also heard the sad news of the death of two of our friends in Grade 13—one had been shot by the Russians; the other had died while on the escape route in 1945. But for me, the way to a new life adventure now stood open, and I entered it with great enthusiasm.

The fall of 1962 brought changes for all of us. While I started to attend the Lakeshore Teachers' College in Etobicoke, our two children changed back to Holy Angels School again, and Heinz became the sole supporter of the family.

Of all my years as teacher, this was the most happy and carefree year for me. I loved "going to school" in the morning at about the same time as the boys, and being home when they arrived back from their school. My classmates at Teachers' College in New Toronto were all high school graduates and just 18 years old, except for one man of about my own age. To my great surprise and delight, I made the same discovery as I had done at Canada Packers—that there was absolutely no discrimination shown by anyone, and I was happy to observe how people, regardless of age, race or national background, got along wonderfully.

There was one day, however, that did reduce me to tears. At the beginning of the day we were told that instead of regular class instructions, we were all required to write an IQ test.

I had never heard of such a thing and wondered what this might be about when the desks were moved apart and we obviously were meant to be unable to look at each others' papers. After a serious instruction of the expected procedure, we were given a booklet of about 10 or 12 pages with questions on different topics and told that we had a given time to finish. At the command "Go!", we had to pick up our pencils and start writing, with the stopwatch ticking the allowable minutes away. From the start, I felt overwhelmed. My English was not yet fluent enough to read and comprehend at the same time. I still tried mostly to translate the meaning first into German and then find the answer in English.

The mathematical questions weren't too bad—at least I knew what the intent of the questions were—but for the rest of the test I soon realized that I just did not have the vocabulary to understand, nor to answer. One after another, the other students handed in their papers, several even before the time was expired until, when the time was up, I was the only one still sitting at my desk, crying out of exasperation. I remember that one of the words I did not know, was "toil". The question had been to find a synonym for it.

The supervising professor was kind and sympathetic and listened to my story of woe. He tried to console me, but I was certain that my dream of becoming a teacher had come to an end and that I would find myself again at the factory, cutting meat for the rest of my life.

Since nothing else was said to me that day, I attended class again the following morning when the same professor called me into the hall and revealed to me that the staff had decided to discount my test due to "special circumstances" and I should worry no longer, just attend regularly and try my best—which I did with gratitude and renewed eagerness. It paid off in the long run. At the end of the year I was one of very few students who were exempted from final written exams and could wave my certificate of completion all the way home.

•

WE WERE SOON SENT OUT to various schools to observe experienced teachers at work, and to learn to teach one or two subjects to children aged six to 14 in Grades 1 to 8. My actual teaching time increased as the weeks went by, and ended in a week-long assignment in the proverbial "little red schoolhouse" in the country, where one teacher taught all grade levels in one classroom.

During this week, the local teacher found accommodations for me with a farm family. On Sunday evening, Heinz and the boys drove me to Milton where the school was located, and on Monday morning, I met the teacher and 28 children of all age groups in a room that reminded me very much of my first school experience as a child.

In the afternoon, I received my teaching assignments for the rest of the week. Having to prepare the lessons for each grade level took me until two or three o'clock in the morning, and while I was teaching, the homeroom teacher observed me. On Friday, one of the college professors arrived and sat in the back of the class for half a day to judge how I was doing. This week was quite stressful; however, the final evaluation turned out to be very positive and I left with the feeling of having survived a great learning experience.

One of my favourite subjects at the college was science, which was often held outdoors. One of our early assignments was to present an original plan that could be taught to young children. At our cottage I had noticed large-leafed green plants that seemed to be crawling with very pretty yellow-black-and-white coloured caterpillars. I decided that children might like to find out what might happen to these creatures, and convinced Heinz to build me a cage of fine mashed wire into which I placed a potted plant with many caterpillars on it. In the public library I discovered that the plant was called milkweed and that only Monarch butterflies would lay their eggs on these leaves. My caterpillar cage was the sensation of the day. It not only earned me an excellent mark but we had the joy of watching the development of the gold-rimmed green cocoons and the hatching of the beautiful butterflies.

Later, in my own Grade 4 class, I repeated this experiment. At the time I had heard of a Professor Urquhardt at the University of Toronto who studied these particular butterflies. The children and I wrote to him, telling him what we had done and received a return letter with a package of very delicate labels and instructions on how to fasten them onto the wings of the butterflies. The professor wanted to know where these insects disappeared to during the winter, and in time we were informed that one of our butterflies had been traced to Mexico. This in turn gave rise to an interesting lesson in geography and increased the interest in the large and small creatures around us.

•

I SPENT MY FIRST YEAR as a fully qualified teacher in a portable classroom with 41 children: 28 in Grade 4 and 13 in Grade 5, at a princely starting salary of $1,800 per year. I had acquired valuable skills in dealing with class discipline and was always trying to find new approaches to keep the interests of the children alive. Several times during the year we performed plays, complete with costumes and an audience which mainly consisted of the principal, Mr. Boulanger, and the school secretary. Sometimes one or two parents were present as well. Holiday themes were always easy to script, but explorer stories and fairy tales provided topics as well.

Each year I took the class to a pet shop, and in the fall to the Royal Winter Fair where we observed the animals and every child would make notes about their various behaviours and needs. The follow-up in the classroom became part of our English, spelling, science, geography, math, health and music lessons. One year we bought two pairs of white mice in the pet shop, to be housed in two small aquariums. Each child in turn brought some food for our new pets, with one difference. The two mice in one aquarium were fed grain, vegetables and some cheese, while the other two received all kinds of "junk food": potato chips, candy, cookies, cake, and so on. Soon, each pair had babies and while the ones with the healthy food thrived, the others remained small and weak and about half of them died. The parent mice did not fare any differently— one pair had shiny, thick white fur; the others became scraggly and thin looking, and we all began to feel sorry for them. The point of the importance of healthy nourishment was made, however, and the children had learned not only new words to read and spell, but a life lesson as well.

Each year, young boys in the separate schools were tested regarding their musical and academic talents. When Garrett was in Grade 5 and Roland in Grade 3, both were recommended to attend the St. Michael's Choir School starting the following September. Both boys had excellent marks and were musically talented. At my insistence, Garrett had started taking accordion lessons at age eight and Roland had picked up playing a small accordion on his own. Both boys also had lovely singing voices. Despite the fact that this would mean another school change, we enrolled the children at this prestigious school without realizing how difficult it would become for the family. Instead of having the school in walking distance from the house, the children now had to be taken by car or bus to the closest streetcar station at the Humber Loop, from where they had a 40-minute streetcar ride through the city to their stop at Bond Street, followed by a walk of several blocks to the new school. Instead of being at home at 3:30 in the afternoon, they now arrived not earlier than 4:30, and sometimes later. Homework was much heavier for both than before, and Garrett told me the school did not permit home-work on the streetcar because the rocking motion spoiled their penman-ship. Homework was inspected, and when they tried to get away with it, they were usually caught "red-handed."

Consequently, the time for play and fun became reduced. Almost every Sunday they were expected to sing in the choir during evening Mass in the Cathedral, which meant that all four of us had to attend the church service instead of spending the weekend at the cottage.[1] How to divide the time to fit in all the activities became a major project.

After one year we all decided that we wanted a simpler, less compli-cated life and the children returned to Holy Angels School. This caused a new and different problem for them, because their mother was a teacher on staff and at times other children would tease them. I tried my best to treat them like any other student in the school. We bought a piano that year and the boys had no difficulty learning to play it.

Though my English had greatly improved, I still did not feel as com-petent as I would have liked. By listening to the discussions of my col-leagues in the lunchroom I discovered there existed the possibility that any person over the age of 25 with a high school diploma could attend the University of Toronto. I could not believe it! Should I, after all this time, and at my ripe old age of 39, finally have one of my great ambitions fulfilled and be able to become a university student? I had to find out what my chances were.

One day in the summer of 1965, I gathered up my courage and went to the registrar's office where, to my great relief and joy, I had no diffi-culty being accepted for the fall evening semester for the grand entrance fee of $35, excluding books. To be somewhat on the safe side, I enrolled in German Literature 101, which I figured I could not fail even if I tried, and in Anthropology 101. It was sheer pleasure attending the lectures and the German course was easy for me, even though I found out that

---

1   Garrett often reminds me that the reason he is a writer today is because of the year he spent at St. Michael's. He had some wonderful teachers, including Miss Mann, whom he credits with his understanding and love of language, and Father Armstrong, who was the Choirmaster at the time.

all the teaching was done in English and the essays had to be written in English as well. However, reading the required German books gave me a great advantage.

I remember the fantastic feeling of privilege and accomplishment, just walking across the university grounds to my classes. One of the teachers from Holy Angels also joined the Anthropology course and we became good friends, studying and working on assignments together, ending with similar marks several times.

Having discovered that I could now follow the instructions and lectures in English, I continued during the following years, until I received my B.A., and eventually in following years, a Masters Degree in Education.

•

THE PRINCIPAL OF THE SCHOOL in which I taught, Holy Angels, approached me at about the same time as I started university classes to ask me to take on a "special education" class rather than teaching a "regular" class. During the 1960s and early 1970s, Toronto was the destination for many immigrants from non-English speaking countries, especially from Italy and Portugal, and the enrolment in schools where these ethnic communities congregated, rose considerably. Many children were unable to follow the prescribed regular curriculum and the idea of establishing special classes for recently-arrived children who were learning English, as well as for physically or mentally handicapped children, began to be put into practice. My principal wanted to start such a class in his school and felt that I would be able to deal with this new challenge. There was one stipulation: I had to take a five-week-long summer course, sponsored by the Ministry of Education, during the holidays, which meant that it would not be possible to spend the summer with the boys at our cottage. After some soul-searching, I gave in to my ambition and agreed to take the class and the course. Again, I found it most interesting to learn about the various handicaps and mental illnesses that children could exhibit, and looked forward to the fall and my new class.

For three years, I taught a "special education" class which never had more than 12 children, aged six to 14, a mixture of boys and girls. For one year when the school did not have an itinerant music teacher, I also taught music in most of the other grades because the teachers did not feel comfortable singing. I, on the other hand, loved to sing and knew a lot of songs I could teach, so we worked out an exchange plan where the regular class teacher would take over my group for a period, while I taught their class a music lesson. From time to time I got a visit from our school superintendent who observed what I was doing and during the following two summers, I again took advanced courses in "special education" to get the specialist certificate.

Promotions

IN JUNE 1969 I WAS OFFERED the position of "special education consultant", later to be called "resource teacher", which I very gladly accepted. In March of that year, my husband Heinz had left us and moved out; I very reluctantly had to agree to the sale of our beloved cottage. By then I had learned to drive a car and had bought myself a used Ford. Garrett attended high school and Roland was in Grade 8. I needed the car personally, but now more so because I had to be mobile in order to drive from school to school to visit and help the Special Ed. teachers with their programs. The district for which I was responsible ran from Highway 401 to the Lakeshore, in all of Etobicoke, and included roughly two dozen schools. I was busy and loved it. The feeling of no longer being closed in by four walls gave me a sense of recaptured freedom, and I began to learn a great deal about how different schools were managed by the principals, whether the atmosphere in a school was positive or negative, and how teachers and students interacted.

Since we no longer owned the cottage, the boys had gotten older and more independent, and money was in short supply, I started to teach summer courses to aspiring Special Ed. teachers. By now I had certainly learned what an IQ test was and often administered one of several kinds to children to identify their needs.

The appointment to this job had a limit of two years, after which time I had to decide whether I wanted to return to the classroom or find something else to do. But I had tasted freedom for too long and met too many interesting people to let myself go back into four closed walls again. I decided to apply for the position of vice principal. After an interview with three superintendents, I landed a position as VP in a downtown Toronto school with classes from kindergarten to Grade 8.

During the next two years, I learned a great deal about how to run a large school from a very capable and kind principal, and gained more and more self-confidence as I realized that the staff of about 40 accepted and respected me, and my leadership. The general rule of the school board was that VPs usually remained two years in one school, and principals five years, before they were transferred to another school to help circulate new ideas.

In the late 1960s and early '70s, many new immigrants with large families arrived in the city from the Azore Islands in Portugal, which in turn caused school enrollment numbers to go up. This was also the reason why my principal at the time had to take over a new school after I had been working with him as a VP for two years. The urgent question for me became: "Where will I be sent?" To my great and very pleasant surprise, I was informed at the end of June 1973 that I was being promoted to become the next principal of the same school. And instead of being transferred after five years, I remained in that school until June 1980, and enjoyed every year of it.

Changes in the Family

DURING MY SECOND YEAR as vice principal, I managed to find and buy another cottage. It was located on a small river in the middle of a forest north of the town of Lindsay.

My two boys had grown up by this time. Garrett decided to study one year in Mexico and Roland was attending Grade 13, the last year of high school. He and I loved to improve the cottage and spent every available weekend there. At that time, I also bought a houseboat together with my new friend, Al, whom I had met at one of the summer courses I took each year.

We all took many beautiful trips through the Kawartha Lakes, rivers and lift locks—one crossing Lake Simcoe to Port Severn at Georgian Bay and back—others with my Aunt Marianne, my mother's sister, who came to visit one summer.

It had been an extremely difficult decision for me to let Garrett leave at the age of 20 to an unknown future in an unknown country with an unknown language, although there would certainly have been no stopping him. Even though I knew he had prepared himself somewhat by taking several weeks of Spanish language lessons, and was enrolled in a school—CIDOC, in the city of Cuernavaca—I cried. He left with a couple, Terri and Ivan, whom he had met through a newspaper advertisement, to drive to Miami and from there to fly to Mexico City. He remained friends with them for many years.

At that time it was not possible for him to telephone me and I was depending on the odd postcard and letters he would write. What gave me strength and confidence were thoughts of my mother and her belief in me when I, as a very young girl, more than once left her behind. I too, knew that Garrett would learn valuable life lessons and survive, just as I had done.

He returned a year later, suntanned, in torn jeans, a dirty T-shirt, but happy. He had met a girl from Toronto in the course they both had taken, and could not wait to introduce her to me with the very definite explanation that he was planning to marry her before the year had ended.

At first I presumed that this was just a passing affair, but as time went on, both he and Debbie became more and more serious about their future, and planned, in spite of my and her parents' objections, their wedding day. In the end there was nothing else for us to do but give them our blessing, and they were married on December 8, 1973, Garrett being 21 and Debbie, 23.

Roland surprised all of us—mainly me—with a relaxed, witty and meaningful speech, which he delivered with great eloquence as a special toast to his brother and the bride. He was 18 at the time and I was more than proud of both my boys.

Heinz, their father, also attended. It was the first time I had seen him in several years. We had some friendly conversation and even danced a waltz together, but I was happy to return home alone. Neither one of us ever married again.

Garrett and Debbie's marriage lasted 17 years with many ups and downs, and the birth of two children, Micah and Lindsay.

Cultural Adjustments

A FEW MONTHS BEFORE THE WEDDING, in September 1973, I began the school year as newly-appointed principal of St. Veronica's, the same school in which I had been a VP the year before. Many memorable events happened during my time there, and I was honoured to share those years with a very capable and loyal staff, and several vice principals.

Most of the families who had immigrated and whose children attended our school came from the Azores, where Portuguese is the official language. During the first few years of my presence in the school, 95 percent of the students were of Portuguese background. The fathers had usually been fishermen, and the mothers had stayed at home looking after the large families. It is small wonder that they became confused with the new, unfamiliar environment, the new language and the loud and fast-moving lifestyle in the largest city in this new country.

Most of the men seemed to find work in the construction industry where they learned to follow basic instructions in English, while the women either stayed at home or found work by cleaning office buildings during the night hours. Very few of them found either the time or the inclination to learn the language of their new country.

Having followed their own traditions and habits all their lives, they continued to do so in Canada. One example of this came to my attention one morning when the social worker and the interpreter—whom I had requested to speak with the parents about their truant children—returned from their home visit and reported the following:

They had found the three children at home in their kitchen where the mother was in the process of preparing a cooked breakfast. While an electric stove stood unused against the wall, the woman had spread an asbestos mat in the middle of the floor, on which she had lit a wood fire. Over it, a pot with some cereal was hanging off a large stick supported by two chairs while the children looked on. The horrified visitors had her extinguish the flames, then explained the danger of her procedure and gave her a lesson on how to use the electric stove. The truancy from school had become of secondary importance and had to be discussed the following day.

Each September at the beginning of the school year, when many children returned from a visit to their home country, I had to request that a group of nurses come to the school to check every child for head lice. The same inspection had to be repeated after the Christmas holidays, when children had come back with lice which they picked up either from visiting relatives, or if they had visited Europe. There were times when not even one child remained in a classroom. They were sent home with explicit instructions and had to return to be rechecked after three days. Since families almost always consisted of several children, all grades in the school were affected. As a staff, we had to develop individual and unusual programs to keep the instruction level at par with the requirements of the curriculum.

Boys in Grades 7 and 8 resented having to attend school. I was told that in the Azores they finished school at age 12 and from then on were considered to be young men who went out on fishing boats with their fathers, and were expected to help support the family. Women were considered not equal to men, and therefore it was beneath a young man's dignity to have to be taught by a woman teacher whose instructions they had to follow.

This was bad enough, but also having a woman as principal was for some beyond endurance. One way to escape this daily regime was to either arrive late in the morning, or not to attend school at all. Of course, something had to be done about this. I found out that several boys liked to go to the local pool halls on Dundas Street and, true to my former police training, I marched into these pool halls several mornings and dragged the boys by their collars back to school with threats of terrible punishment. Word got around; the pool halls were avoided, but lateness and truancy continued.

Another reason for non-attendance was the fact that the parents needed the children to go with them for various practical or financial reasons. One was that they had to pick earthworms during the night, which would be sold to anglers or which they would use themselves. Of course in the morning, they all were tired and stayed home. In the spring, the mothers and children went to collect fresh dandelion plants to eat in salads, or the mothers had found jobs as cleaners in high-rise office buildings and took their children with them rather than leaving them alone at home.

Because of my background in Special Education, our school was assigned to accept several classes with children who needed additional help, whether it was to learn English or to receive special attention because of behavioural, mental or intellectual difficulties.

One 12-year-old boy who had been tested and assigned to one of the special classes exhibited particularly aggressive behaviour. He felt that he was too old to go to school and wanted, at the very least, to have a man as a teacher. As not many male teachers were available in our school system, he had been properly placed, but with a female teacher.

One morning after he refused to attend to an assignment and the teacher demanded that he follow her instructions, he picked up the large typewriter in the room and threw it at her in a fit of rage. It fell on her foot but did not cause serious injury; however, she was at the end of her patience and angrily came to the office to demand that the boy be removed from her class. I did feel that she was justified and that the boy had to calm down and learn to respect women. Following prescribed procedure, I decided to suspend him for three days, had the teacher prepare homework for him, then called the interpreter to notify the parents and to take him home. The instructions for the parents were not to let him play outside for the next three days, but insist on the completion of the assigned homework.

The following day I asked his younger sister how her brother was behaving at home, whereupon she informed me quite innocently that he was alright; her parents had to go out to work and her father had chained him up in the basement where he could not get into trouble. I was horrified and immediately reported this to the social worker who was assigned to our school and who arrived promptly. We had to find the father at work, who came to the school furious, blaming us for having these crazy rules that he tried to follow exactly by preventing his son from running out of the house, and now that we did not agree with his methods, we had made him lose some hours of work and wages.

The outcome of this situation was that the social worker brought the boy back to school. I arranged for him, and from then on, for any subsequent culprits, to sit in an isolated room near the office during school hours, without recess, but with lots of work to do. I was also able to buy a large, used punching bag from a fitness gym, which was hung in the same room and children with angry outbursts were encouraged to punch it until they felt better. It was worth the money I spent on it.

Motivating parents to come to parent-teacher meetings was almost impossible, and those who did come spoke little or no English. I hired a young Portuguese-speaking secretary, Christine, who was worth her weight in gold, as an interpreter and office manager. A permanent interpreter also was assigned to our school, and at certain occasions we needed three, four or more.

To get parents to teacher interviews, one idea that occurred to me—and with which I had great success—was to involve the Portuguese priest of the community in my conspiracy. He was a young, energetic and enthusiastic man, who helped us to find a place that rented Portuguese movies. When I was planning a parent-teacher evening to discuss the progress of the children (or the lack of it) with the parents, I let it be known through flyers and church announcements that a "Free

Portuguese Movie" was to be shown on a certain evening. Each time, our gymnasium was filled with parents. Once we had them in the building, I went in front of them and said, "Yes, we are going to show you the movie, but not before you hear a few things that I have to say...." Then when the movie ended, we did not open the doors again until the teachers had a chance to talk with the parents of the children in their class. To appease the parents and to establish a non-threatening atmosphere, I made sure a coffee and donut table was set up, to which everyone had free access. At that time, a small amount of money would buy a lot of treats.

Some of the newly arrived children suffered from homesickness. One sunny afternoon shortly before the final bell rang, a policeman arrived at the school with two nine-year-old boys. We had noticed that they had been absent in the afternoon, presumed that they were truant and had tried unsuccessfully to contact the home. Here they arrived with tears running down their dirty little faces, standing with a guilty look on either side of a stern, uniformed man of the law. To our amazement, we were told that they had decided to return to Portugal, had untied a rowboat at the shore of Lake Ontario and had started to row "back home". The harbour police had spotted the boat on the water and proceeded to quash the valiant, adventurous attempt of the boys to reach the Azores, unceremoniously handing them over to the local police.

The teacher had a good reason to teach a very valuable lesson on local and global geography to her class.

At home, a very happy event took place. Roland, now age 30, got married to his fiancée, Wanda, on August 4, 1985. He had travelled the continent and some parts of Europe, had attained his MBA at the University of London, Ontario, and was now in the process of establishing his own business, as his brother had already done. After Garrett's wedding, Heinz had kept loose contact with the boys, and again attended the ceremony. My brother Juergen, whose first wife had died, also attended with his second wife, Winnie, from Denver, Colorado, where they still live.

Another Change of Schools

IT WAS CUSTOMARY THROUGHOUT the school board that principals would be transferred to another school after they had worked five years in a given location. Such a change was thought to be of benefit to both the principal—to prevent boredom or monotony—and to his present school, to provide new ideas and a fresh approach to the program.

I still had many good ideas to try out, and as fate would have it, I remained another two years at the same school, a total of nine in all: two as VP and seven as principal. This was because an extensive renovation of the building had begun in my eighth year, which I needed to see through to the end. During my ninth year, a new superintendent took over our region, and he wanted as few changes as possible during his first year.

However, after a memorable goodbye ceremony, I left the school in 1980 to take on the assignment of a still larger one with about 800 children, a staff of 50 teachers, as well as support personnel and a schoolyard filled with portable classrooms.

This school happened to be located in a district with a lesser Portuguese population, but one of my surveys disclosed that our children came from a background representing 23 different languages. This is to say that they spoke English in school only, and in the afternoon went back to a home where another language was spoken.

I had a very capable vice principal, and this time a secretary who spoke Italian, which was of help in many instances. Again, a building program became the cause for my lengthened stay in this school for six years, instead of only five.

Exceptionally good memories remain with me about these years: the cohesiveness and comradeship of the staff, the improvement of various programs, especially in regard to our school library and the special education classes, and successful parent involvement. Of course there were days when my hair grew a few grey streaks.

I recall days when I had to deal with the incompetence of a certain teacher, or when one of the children was forgotten on the Toronto Islands after an outdoor excursion, or when a high school teenager collapsed and died in our gym which the school board had rented out for community evening sports programs.

With much regret I had to transfer for my last assignment to yet another school, this time for a duration of only four years, which ended with my retirement at age 65.

A new challenge awaited me in this so-called "French Immersion School". Not only was French taught to select "gifted" students, most of whom were bussed in every day, but the classrooms were built on a new, experimental "open" concept. Originally each room had looked like a very big hall, housing four teachers with her children, one class in each of the four corners. By the time I arrived, the building was about 15 years old and, on the recommendation of former principals and teachers, had finally been somewhat modified by the erection of partitions. Now, at least the visible distraction would be minimized, if not the noise level.

A talented, efficient vice principal made my transition easy. During my stay, he greatly helped to improve the music program by producing the musical *The Music Man*, and by accompanying many events with his guitar and beautiful voice. After three years he was transferred to be replaced with a very capable young lady.

The school had several other special programs, such as an instrumental program, an experimental program for three-year old children, and several special education programs. For intermediate Grade 7 and 8 students from our own and surrounding schools, there was a program that taught cooking and sewing as well as wood and metal work. This meant that I, too, had a lot to learn, and many adjustments to make.

My teaching career ended with two memorable ceremonies: one with all the children and teachers in the school, the other beginning with a church service and ending in a party with colleagues, family and friends from the past and the present.

CHAPTER FOURTEEN

Spiritual and Worldly Journeys

By the time of my first transfer to another school as principal, I had completed my BA and Masters Degree in Education at the University of Toronto, in the evening program.

At the university and at meetings and conventions, of which I attended many, I met many interesting people. Among them were three ladies who became lifelong friends, all three of them also principals. The first one I met, Mary Ellen, was a born Canadian, had three adopted children, was—and still is—kind, outspoken and very active in our teacher organization. The second, Kay, I met at the principal's course. Of Japanese background, her parents immigrated to British Columbia before World War II, and she grew up in a Japanese internment camp in Canada. My third friend, Shirley, moved to Toronto from Trinidad with her husband and two daughters. All three could write a very interesting book about their own life story. The four of us have remained friends long after our retirements.

Another most interesting person I met was an Austrian woman, Hildegard, who had been in Canada longer than I. During the last painful year of my marriage I frequently gave her a ride home from the university courses we both attended, and was introduced by her to the writings of Paramahansa Yogananda. His book, *Autobiography of a Yogi*, became the beginning of my spiritual studies. It gave me a tremendous feeling of hope, confidence and purpose, and caused me to seek out more sources of spiritual understanding and insight.

As it is said in the Bible: "Seek and ye shall find." Suddenly, doors opened that had been invisible to me until then. I enrolled in two long-distance courses of the Self Realization Fellowship (SRF)and studied the monthly lessons diligently over a period of about two years. I started to meditate. Both my sons also read Yogananda's book and started to ask pertinent questions. Our lives began to change in a positive way. The SRF lessons are still filed in binders on one of my bookshelves.

Regular searches through bookstores led me to several "Eckankar"[1] books by Paul Twitchell, including *The Far Country, Dialogues With the Master*, and others. From the Eckankar group I also purchased individual lessons and studies. These, however, seemed a little strange and far-fetched to me, though they broadened my outlook and made my quest ever more urgent.

The next door that opened came through an advertisement in the Toronto Star newspaper, telling readers of a visit to Toronto's Convocation Hall of a man by the name of Hugh Lynn Cayce. He was the son of a modern-day psychic named Edgar Cayce, who apparently had been able during his lifetime[2] to heal many people and make prophetic statements while in a trance state. I had never heard of either of them.

I was one of the hundreds of attendees at this slide presentation given by Mr. Cayce. He related psychic experiments he had observed in Russia of a woman who could move coins with her mind, and mentioned Uri Geller of Israel, who, it was said, could bend spoons with his mind. Whether these claims were true or not, the point was made: the human mind is a powerful yet unexplored tool we all possess. At the end we all were made aware of a group in Toronto called the Association for Research and Enlightenment (ARE), which was open for membership to anyone who was interested. Several book titles were mentioned that

---

1   Eckankar is an ancient Indian science of secret worlds, invisible to our physical senses.

2   Edgar Cayce lived from 1877 to 1945.

would make the reader familiar with the life of Edgar Cayce.

I purchased them all the next day.[3]

A whole new world began to open up for me. Ideas I had never thought of suddenly caused me to look at my own life from a different angle, and reinforced my understanding of what I had read in the Yogananda teachings and what I remembered from the Christian teachings in my youth. I felt the need to discuss these new insights with like-minded, searching people, and joined an ARE group that met at someone's home once a week, to read and discuss the only book Edgar Cayce had ever written, *A Search For God*.

My son Roland, 17 or 18 at the time, still lived at home, and on my enthusiastic urging also became involved. I volunteered our home for his weekly meeting, while I attended my meeting elsewhere. And so our regular weekly ARE meetings started.

A few times the membership changed slightly, by a person leaving or someone new joining, and after about two years the remaining sincere searchers of both groups combined for another six months or so. At that time, Roland and the other young people moved, or went to university or college or found jobs elsewhere. Three older women remained: Isa, Joyce and I.

It was the early 1970s and for the next 35 years, the three of us met without fail each Wednesday in one of our living rooms and studied. We went on to read all books by Jane Roberts, several by Ouspensky, Gurdjieff and many by Joel Goldsmith, in addition to the Bible in different translations and other authors of spiritual writings. Usually one of us read aloud, while we all freely interrupted and discussed valid points; sometimes we only managed one paragraph the whole night. Our meetings became longer and longer, often lasting until 3 o'clock in the morning, and we selected Friday nights as a better choice. Friday also suited us bettter because another door opened in 1975 or 1976: we discovered Unity Church Of Truth in Toronto.

---

3   *There Is A River*, by Thomas Sugrue; *Many Mansions* by Gina Cerminara; *Yoga, Youth and Reincarnation* and *Edgar Cayce, The Sleeping Prophet*, both by Jess Stern.

Unity

UNITY CHURCH HAD TWO EXCEPTIONAL ministers at that time: Jim Sherman and Ed Rabel. Forever will I be grateful to these inspiring two men for having clarified and emphasized the teachings of Jesus for me. I came to realize the value of the brilliant, unique, spiritual and universal psychological teachings of Jesus, and how these could be translated into our modern-day language and understanding. They became an invaluable, priceless help in my own life. [4]

For many years, Isa, Joyce and I attended a learning class one evening each week, in addition to the two services every Sunday morning, one at 9 a.m. with Rev. Ed Rabel, the next at 11 a.m. with Rev. Jim Sherman. Inspired by them, I enrolled one summer in a two-week course at Unity Village, stayed in one of their cottages with some like-minded young women, and did not miss a single one of the lectures that were given by various teachers.

Though the Fillmores wrote many excellent and uplifting books, of which I own many, the credit for my enthusiasm and eagerness to learn more about these life changing attitudes goes to the delivery of the teaching by our two Toronto ministers.

For me, the most impressive and important insight I gained was the unshakable, conscious awareness and trust that I exist as eternal Spirit in a temporal human form, within the constant and continuing presence of God, and that this is true for everyone else. Just as fish are surrounded by water, not even realizing that water is their life-giving element, so I and every other human being are surrounded by this element we call God, the Presence and Power that is the source and sustenance of our life. Charles Fillmore put it in the form of a prayerful invocation:

4   Unity Church began as a non-denominational church with Charles and Myrtle Fillmore in the 1880s in Kansas City. It has long since developed into its own community with its own post office as Unity Village, Missouri, 64065, www.unityonline.org. For interested Toronto based readers the address in this city is: Unity Church of Truth, 173 Eglinton Ave. West, Toronto, ON, www.unitytoronto.ca. The minister still is Rev. James Sherman.

I am now in the presence of pure Being and immersed in the
   Holy Spirit of life, love and wisdom.
I acknowledge Thy presence and Thy power, O blessed Spirit;
in Thy divine wisdom now erase my mortal limitations
and from Thy pure substance of love bring into manifestation
   my world, according to Thy perfect law.

I always try to put myself and all my worldly affairs in perspective by declaring "Divine Order". I have learned that thoughts are things, and that thoughts held in mind produce after their kind, and many more attitude-altering truths which I always try to remember and live by. There are too many to mention here and impossible to fit into the correct and convincing words. Truth and the unfailing power of love can only be learned by experience. We need to find out for ourselves that this teaching works.

Our awakening may start with a simple thing, such as asking the ever-present Higher Power—usually called God, but the "name" is of no importance—in sincerity and trust, for a parking spot—and it will be there. In the Bible Jesus tells us to "Ask and it shall be given you, seek and you shall find, knock and it shall be opened unto you."[5] Unless we emotionally desire to "find", it will elude us. When we know, that we finally *know* that we know, then we are certain of Life, Love, Wisdom and Truth. There will be no more room for fear, anger, guilt or any other negativity. Ed Rabel used to refer to it as "useless, unnecessary suffering".

I have been forever grateful that fate channelled me in the direction of becoming a teacher in the Catholic school system. The very fact that it is based on Christian teachings and values allowed me to freely talk about God and Jesus. I was able to practice, by conscious effort, Christian truths, and to try to be an example through my words and actions to children and adults alike. I was always glad that I could share with the children and the teachers on staff, and often with parents, what I had learned, or better, what light bulb had gone on in my understanding. It never contradicted basic Catholic teachings; it just made it more

5   Matthew 7:7

understandable and applicable to life in our time.

Had I entered the public school system, where religious teachings unfortunately are no longer allowed, I probably would have become frustrated and unhappy, and would soon have had reason to look for another occupation.

In one of his lessons at Unity, Jim Sherman declared that a Unity minister has fulfilled his calling, if, like a good parent, he or she can "send" the student out again "into the world" to continue to follow his or her own Inner Teacher and His guidance. After about six or seven years, my two friends and I felt that we had learned as much as was possible by going to the Unity lessons. Ed Rabel had returned to Unity Village in Kansas and a few new ministers did not seem to have his spiritual insight and teaching ability. Our attendance became less regular, until, after Isa also moved away, we stopped going to the classes and services.

What we never did stop, however, were our regular private meetings one evening per week during which we continued to read and discuss spiritual writings, setting certain disciplines for ourselves to practice before our next meeting and, as we called it, "charge our spiritual batteries" for the coming week. Joyce and I are still, in 2013, following this established practice and though from time to time we change our topics slightly, we always remember, that we are the "I AM", living in the "NOW", knowing that Love, Faith, Forgiveness, and Gratitude, as taught by Jesus, are the most important ways to live by on this three-dimensional planet. The teachings of Unity changed my disposition and mental attitude towards life forever.

Travel and Retirement

I RETIRED AT AGE 65 FROM a 28-year teaching career, which happened to be in June of 1990. The staff of my last school, together with my two talented sons, arranged for a very memorable "goodbye party" attended by about 200 people, my family, colleagues, teachers and many friends that had crossed my path over the years. Garrett and Roland presented a slideshow depicting my life and Roland had engaged some of his musical friends to perform as a live band, with himself on the accordion.

Thanks to a good pension program, I have had no financial difficulties. Some savings accounts allowed me to support the expenses for my newly acquired pleasure in traveling.

During the last six years of my principalship I had volunteered as a member on the already-existing "travel committee for principals". It had become customary that interested principals travelled as a group during the annual March break to different countries at their personal expense. For many years I did not participate because I felt the costs were too high. However, in the early 1980s, when a trip was planned to France and my son Roland just happened to be studying in Holland, I decided to join the group and in so doing, meet at the same time with Roland, who was able to come to France for a few days. That is when the "travel bug" bit me.

The principals' committee decided that these excursions were to be held every second year, but were to last two weeks instead of only one. The purpose became an educational one, with the goal of studying the school systems in the countries to be visited.

From that time on I did not miss a single opportunity to travel with our group, except during one year, when I broke my foot just prior to our planned departure for Germany, Switzerland and northern Italy.

The countries we visited always received us as official representatives of the Canadian school system, and treated us royally. The school visits were previously arranged and an interpreter was present, when necessary. It was most interesting and eye opening to experience a day in a school of a foreign country. We always took a gift for each school, usually a large book with photographs of Canada, which one of us ceremoniously presented to the respective principal.

Even after my retirement I remained on the planning committee, until the school board cancelled the program in the mid-1990s. The travels to all these foreign countries belong to some of my fondest memories.

I always shared accommodations with my Japanese friend Kay, and the two of us many times undertook our own explorational excursions when the group preferred a rest period or visited some restaurant. We came to visit every continent, except Australia and Antarctica; that will have to wait until my next reincarnation.

It is impossible to say which country impressed me most, or which of them was my favourite trip. Roland was able to accompany me to Hong Kong, where he bought the engagement ring for his future wife, Wanda. The floating village of junks in the Aberdeen district impressed on us again, as many times before and after in other countries, how fortunate we are to live in Canada. The view of the city from the high mountain, the Victoria Peak, was breathtaking.

In Japan we explored Tokyo, took the bullet train to Kyoto and saw the pagodas and shrines in Nikko.

Thailand's Imperial Palace looked like an enchanting place from a fairy tale book and the floating market had the most delicious bananas I ever ate, having just been picked by trained monkeys from high trees. I will never forget the impressive, artistic temple complexes on the islands of Java and Bali.

In Jordan we rode on horseback through the gorge to Petra, the city hewn into the walls of quartz cliffs, and in Greece, we tried our luck at the oracle of Delphi. Malaysia and Singapore visits were combined at another time, as were Spain and Morocco. The pyramids in Egypt, the valley of the kings, the temples of Luxor and Karnak as well as the many historical and biblical sites in Israel, are unforgettable.

Our visit in each country would deserve a detailed, written report, as was the case with China. Again we stayed in Hong Kong for a short time and flew from there to the various destinations: Shanghai, with the western, modern influence; Bejing with the Imperial Palace and a side trip to the Great Wall; Xian with the unbelievable army of clay soldiers, until we finally reached Guilin after a five-hour boat trip on the river Lee, passing through the "sugar loaf" mountains which are often depicted on Chinese silk cloth and wall decorations.

Some of these trips took place during my last decade of work, the others after my retirement. Though the program was eventually cancelled, my travels continued. I have since been three times in Alaska, once again in Israel and twice in Hawaii; with my friend Kay in Ecuador, the Galapagos Islands and Peru; in Holland, Italy, Austria, Switzerland, England, Scotland, and of course, several times in all parts of Germany and the U.S.A.

Now, at 88, I travel with my son Garrett and his life-partner Melanie to a Caribbean vacation every chance we get, most recently to see hump-back whales in Los Cabos. Once a year, for the past several years, Garrett and Melanie have taken me with them during their holidays. They like going to the warm, southern climate in the Caribbean Islands or Mexico, preferably during our winter time, where Garrett can scuba dive and Melanie can read her favourite novel on the beach, and where I gladly join her. While the preparations for a flight and the airport procedures have become too arduous for me, the three of us have fun taking full benefit of the preferential service offered when personnel take note of my cane. Our next trip is back to Cozumel in just a few weeks, where I will not be the oldest one in the group. We will rendezvous with some of Melanie's friends from Alberta, one of whom is 92. Garrett jokes that we will have wheelchair races through the airport.

•

ONE VERY SAD EVENT HAPPENED on November 30, 2010, when Garrett's daughter, Lindsay, my granddaughter, very unexpectedly died. Her health had not been good after she had fallen a few years prior and broken her coccyx, but nobody expected her to be suffering from an un-diagnosed heart condition, which was discovered to have been the cause of her sudden death.

There is no life without sorrow and we do well to humbly accept what is given us. It has been said that the only constant in life is change, and I can wholeheartedly attest to that. I also believe that nothing is pre-sented to a person without that person also being given the strength to deal with it, however difficult it may be.

Each person we meet can become a mirror of ourselves and thus a teacher; we would never be aware of another's "faults" if those same qualities did not also reside within us. Each situation we find ourselves in is there for us to learn. What the lesson in each case may be, is for us to discover.

•

WE LIVED IN OUR FIRST HOUSE on Zorra Street for 22 years. After Garrett's marriage he moved to Oakville, then to Toronto and finally to Elora. Roland also married and moved with his family from Toronto to Hespeler and finally to Oakville. Both my sons have built their own businesses, and are working independently in their fields of expertise.

In 1978, I was able to sell the property on Zorra Street for $62,000 and bought a much larger, bungalow-style house in another area of Etobicoke. I lived there for 12 years before also moving to Hespeler, partly to be closer to my two youngest grandchildren, Jessica and Conrad, who are Roland's children, and partly because I was drawn to the idea of living in a rural environment again.

While there, I invited my remaining old school friends from Germany to visit me for the 50th reunion of our high school graduation. All of them accepted and when they arrived, I was prepared with a detailed program for their two-week stay. Three of them found lodging in Roland's house, while the other five stayed with me. We rented a van and for the first week explored by way of day trips the neighbouring area: Hamilton, Niagara Falls, Guelph, the Elora Gorge and other small places. The second week I proudly drove them through the southern part of Ontario, via Wasaga, Muskoka, Algonquin Park to Ottawa, back through Peterborough, Kingston and, of course, Toronto. For two weeks, we all relived our teenage years with adventurous enthusiasm.

My citizenship in Hespeler was of short duration, lasting only two years. I found it very difficult to readjust to the country lifestyle. Though I had two memorable years with Jessica and Conrad, who were seven and five years old respectively, I decided to return to "the big city". Since 1994, I have lived in a raised bungalow in Mississauga at the outskirts of Toronto, and hope to remain here, until "the bell tolls" for me.

My backyard, with a gazebo and two small fish ponds, replaces a cottage environment and keeps me busy and contented in the summer. I also often take the one-hour drive to Elora, where Garrett and Melanie have opened a Bed and Breakfast. Their one acre property is located directly on the Grand River, which offers excellent fly-fishing, and the house has undergone many renovations since they took it over in 2003. Their garden likes my help and supervision. I call it my private resort.

Roland and his family also left Cambridge to settle down in Oakville, about 20 kilometres west of where I live. His children have grown up, and after finishing their university studies were, like me, bitten by the "travel bug". Jessica eventually decided to become a teacher like her mother, her grandmother, her great-grandmother and two aunts. Conrad at this point, is still travelling through the world and will have to decide his future direction whenever he is ready. Micah, Garrett's son, lives independently in an apartment in Burlington, Ontario. I visit with all of them frequently, together or individually, depending on who is available at the time.

All of us, as a family, get together regularly at various festivities. I, now being "old and grey", have the benefit of mostly being invited to my sons' places—they know that I no longer like to cook.

From time to time, I still meet with some of my former "teacher friends" and continue to enjoy my retirement every day.

To conclude my story, I am extremely grateful for all the life lessons that have been presented to me. Although at times they have been trying and very difficult, even frightening, they have formed my character, my spiritual conviction, my attitude, and my behaviour. I have been blessed with a wonderful family, in which I also include my brother and the members of his family.

At all times throughout my life, I have been guided to be in the right place at the right time. I feel was given the gift of insight to see and take the opportunities that life presented me, and have been graced with a protection that has enabled me to keep going forward. These gifts have always been provided, in Divine Order, by my invisible friends, my Guardian Angels.

~

ACKNOWLEDGEMENTS

I have often been asked over the years by my children and the friends I met in North American about my past life in Europe, especially during the war years. Sometimes I came to feel disheartened at having to talk repeatedly about those sad and dreadful experiences, as they always brought back emotions that are difficult to deal with. I decided to put in writing my memories about myself and our family, so that my children and grandchildren would have some knowledge of their ancestors prior to the end of the Second World War. When I began to write down these memories of my life, I never intended to do it in book form.

Little did I realize how interested my sons, Garrett and Roland, would become in the story. I am grateful to both of them for getting me set up with a computer and helping me with the technical knowledge that made the writing process faster and easier. When I thought I was finished, they kept encouraging me to continue the story beyond our arrival in Canada.

My older son, Garrett, foresaw the completion in book form, and without his time and considerable contribution to reading, editing, design and layout, this book would never have seen the light of day. He is the author of the poem at the front of this book, written in 1976 to mark the birth of his son. He knows he has my gratitude.

I also wish to thank one friend in particular, Marie Ellen Lawless, who often encouraged me to write about my Canadian experiences, especially during the 28 years from school teacher to principal. Finally, I thank my friend and Garrett's partner, Melanie Ward, for proofreading the manuscript "with a fine-tooth comb", and catching all the many inconsistencies and spelling mistakes that the rest of us missed.

ABOUT THE AUTHOR

Maria-Dorothea Klassen grew up in a small village not far from the Baltic Sea, in an eastern region of Germany which is now part of modern-day Poland. Through her power of will, smart-wittedness and some well-timed help from her lifelong Angels, she managed as a teenager to escape from the advancing Russian army at the end of World War II, and build a new life in Canada.

Her ability to lead others demonstrated itself early in life. She was mayor of a village at age 20, outwitted bureaucrats and soldiers enroute to freedom, worked as a Red Cross nurse, plainclothes police detective, meat packer, Avon salesperson, special education teacher, elementary school principal, and, of course, mother. She did all this while engendering throughout her life the love and respect of friends, co-workers, and certainly, family.

Arriving in Canada with no knowledge of English, she advanced herself through desire and education, and as witnessed by this manuscript, achieved a high level of proficiency in her adopted language. She began writing about her life experiences while in her 70s.

Dorothea is fond of saying, and singing, "I'm alert, alive, awake, enthusiastic." She is certainly all of that. Today, she drives a new car to visit family and friends, and at age 89, lives in her own house, with beautiful gardens and a fish pond, in Mississauga, Ontario.

CPSIA information can be obtained at www.ICGtesting.com
Printed in the USA
LVOW05s0118170614

390283LV00006B/24/P

9 780993 703409